Quilts
for Fabric
Lovers

ALEX ANDERSON

C&T PUBLISHING

Edited by Harold Nadel
Technical information edited by Joyce Engels Lytle
Cover and book design and electronic illustrations by "Rose Sheifer-
    Graphic Productions," Walnut Creek, CA
Photography by Sharon Risedorph
Author Photo by Adair Anderson

With thanks to my family for their support, and to those who make our journey possible—
Thank you, Diana and Harold.

Library of Congress Cataloging-in-Publication Data
Anderson, Alex (Alexandra Sladky). 1955-
      Quilts for fabric lovers / Alex Anderson.
          p.   cm.
      ISBN 0-914881-87-6
      1. Patchwork—Patterns.   2. Patchwork quilts   I. Title.
    TT835. A52   1994
      746.9 ' 7—dc20   94-15499

Published by C&T Publishing
P. O. Box 1456
Lafayette, California 94549

Printed in Hong Kong by Regent Publishing Services Limited
10 9 8 7 6 5 4 3 2 1

Table of Contents

Introduction 6

    Basic Design Techniques: Choosing a Block 7

    Creative Use of Fabric 7

        Choosing Fabric 7

        The Tests 11

            Light to Dark 11

            Character of Print 12

            Color Groups 13

        Further Fabric Hints 14

    Design 18

        Using Different-Sized Blocks 18

        Secondary Patterns 19

        Block Rotation 19

        Block Combination 20

        Block Within Block 20

        Repeating Block Parts 21

        Humor and Surprises 21

        Lemonade 21

    Laying Out the Quilt 21

        Borders 22

    General Instructions 23

    The Finishing Touches 23

    Quick Cutting Magic Numbers 24

The Quilts

    Maple Leaf 26

    Postage Stamp 30

    Double Sawtooth Star 34

    Saltbox House 38

    Fishing with Pop-Pop 42

    Sailboat 47

    Cherry Basket 52

Template Patterns 58

Introduction

Discover the creative quilter within you! You've heard the creative voice inside you crying, "Help, get me out of here!" You are tired of copying other people's quilts—trying to find exactly the same fabric, becoming frustrated, and depriving yourself of creative decisions. The thought of being creative can be frightening, but with just a few simple ideas and guidelines you can let your own spirit emerge.

When I started teaching, my primary focus was to lead students to sharpen their piecing skills. I soon recognized that piecing techniques were secondary to the magic and joy, as well as the frustration, of fabric selection and basic design choices. Most quiltmakers pride themselves upon their frequent pilgrimages to fabric stores—and the creative ways they hide their stash. (Have you tried cereal boxes?) However, when the time comes to use their collection, instant insecurity descends upon them. In frustration, they end up making an exact replica of someone else's quilt: another trip to the fabric store, this time to match each little piece in the photograph they're copying, rather than starting by pulling from their collection, then adding great new pieces from the quilt shop. Whenever I find inspiration in someone else's quilt, I use it as a catalyst and springboard for my own creativity.

During one class, after I had given a long-winded explanation of fabric choices, discussing just what works, a student asked, "But what are we making?" My answer was, "I don't know: it's your quilt; let's see where your pattern and fabric choices take you." To start without an idea of exactly where you are going is unsettling for those who have not yet enjoyed that journey. But, for those who have, it is an exciting exploration into the unknown. Through this process we can begin to grow and become confident quiltmakers.

In this book, I will give you basic guidelines in fabric selection and design techniques that will forever change your approach to quiltmaking. With a little manipulation and imagination, you will learn how to bring new life to even the simplest block. Simple traditional blocks have the greatest appeal for me. Through my years of quiltmaking, I have developed several tricks that produce exciting results. Using the guidelines, you can bring sparkle to the most basic block.

In this book we will explore seven different quilts, with complete instructions for construction. Each quilt celebrates the use of many fabrics and exemplifies manageable design techniques that you can incorporate into your own future quilts. I have rated the quilts on ease of construction. If you are a beginner, you may want to start with the Maple Leaf, then work your way through the more challenging quilts. This book celebrates creativity with simple blocks, without complicated piecing. You will learn how to make a quilt from basic blocks, but one that has your name written all over it. Even with the most basic instructions, never forget my Golden Rule: *All rules were meant to be broken—at least, on special occasions*! I give you some guidelines, but trust yourself. If it looks like it's time to break the rules, do it! Remember, the design manipulations are only guides to use when appropriate.

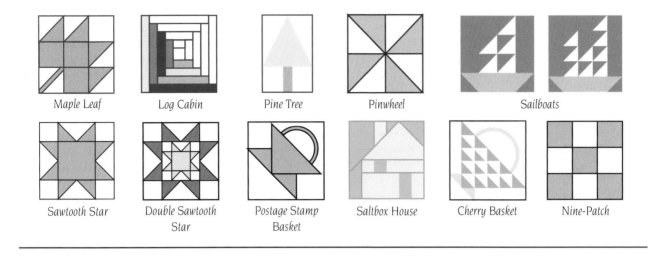

Maple Leaf

Log Cabin

Pine Tree

Pinwheel

Sailboats

Sawtooth Star

Double Sawtooth Star

Postage Stamp Basket

Saltbox House

Cherry Basket

Nine-Patch

Basic Design Techniques: Choosing a Block

First, you must choose your block: keep it simple. I like working with the classics, because they have familiar, universal appeal. In this book I have chosen to work with the blocks above, appealing and fairly straight-forward in their construction.

Many of these blocks have several variations. I like to work with the simpler ones. I enjoy the process of designing, not suffering through a piecing puzzle. You may want to substitute your own block choices. (See page 24 for Quick Cutting Magic Numbers.) Pick a block you are familiar with or have worked with before. The design techniques and fabric options will work beautifully with any block. Use your favorite block and let your creative spirit emerge.

Once I have decided which block or blocks I am going to use, I go to my basic guidelines for choosing fabric. Then the creative process begins. As your quilt takes form, be willing to change direction if necessary. Do not lock yourself into a preconceived finished product; let the quilt take on a life of its own. If you don't keep your plans flexible, you might as well be going on a vacation trip, finding out that a great fabric store is along the route, and refusing to stop because it wasn't in your original plan. What a missed opportunity!

Creative Use of Fabric

CHOOSING FABRIC

Fabric is the biggest decision we have to make. For many people it is a paralyzing experience. I can remember my early terrors in the quilt shop. How did other people choose their fabrics so easily? I must confess that, even with an art degree, I felt very insecure. Through many years of teaching, during which I have had to deal with other people's fabric, I have come up with a set of foolproof guidelines. Follow these simple rules of fabric selection and you too will become a fearless fashion fabriholic. I now consider every bolt of fabric a potential candidate for a quilt: if I think a fabric is ugly, I am ignorant of its use!

I like to work with many fabrics. The more variety in my quilt, the better. It is important to keep an up-to-date fabric stash. Every time I visit my local quilt shop, I check out the new lines of fabric. Each season, you will discover there is a new look to the fabric. On one visit you might find that all the greens have yellow in them, but during your last visit the greens all looked a little blue. This month you might see that plaids are hot, yet two months ago the look was botanical. It is very common for the prints to change frequently. When you see a fabric that you love, get it! That special piece of fabric might not be there the next time you visit your favorite quilt shop. You will find that different stores carry different selections, so visiting stores on a regular basis is a valuable investment of your time. Allow yourself to start collecting a palette of fabric: it's okay to buy fabric but not use it in the quilt you thought it was meant for; it might just be the piece that rescues your next quilt. By collecting fabrics from season to season, your quilts will lose the pre-packaged look and will emerge with your style. If you are a new quilter, you can still achieve an independent look by following my guidelines. (I have also found that quilters are very giving people and will help out by sharing their fabric with friends!)

Focus Fabric

This is a tried and true approach to fabric selection. Look for a large-scale print with several different colors, from which you will pull your other fabric choices. The colors in the focus fabric will set the look of the quilt. When deciding which fabric to use, make sure that there are variations of each color represented in the print. For example, if the fabric has leaves, check that the leaves have several greens. You must become a fabric detective, looking for all of the colors you see, and not just the ones you feel comfortable with. After careful scrutiny you might be surprised at some of the colors you find. Once you have identified the colors in your focus fabric, start pulling out several bolts of fabric from each color group. Buy not only the fabrics that you are in love with; add little amounts of those that you are uncomfortable with. Some of the fabrics may not appeal to you, but use them. You aren't decorating your house, you are expanding your knowledge of fabric! I used this technique in the Maple Leaf, Double Sawtooth Star, and Cherry Basket quilts.

Holiday or Seasonal

This is a safe way to start, with guaranteed results. Think of your favorite holiday or season. I received lots of joy and ended up with a smashing July birthday quilt when I chose this route for the Sailboat quilt. Once I decided that I was going with July, I used every scrap of red, white, and blue possible. When you work with an established color set, it is fun to watch unlikely fabric combinations work together and sing. One principle for choosing fabric for holiday quilts is to use a combination of a few specific holiday prints mixed with fabrics from the color group for the look you want. If you use only fabric with seasonal prints your quilt can become confusing, because there isn't a resting place for your eye. To mix and match with fabric from different collections is the solution. This is also an excellent way to become comfortable making unusual fabric combinations. The results are personal and less commercial looking.

Representational and Theme Fabrics

Sometimes the story you want to tell, or the blocks you decide to use, will determine your fabric choices. The Fishing with Pop-Pop quilt uses fabrics that represent the blocks realistically. For the trees, I looked specifically for greens that had foliage prints, and for browns that looked like bark. For the lake I hunted for fabric that resembled water. This is an instructive approach to picking fabric, because it forces you to look at the print unemotionally: it is no longer important whether or not you like the fabric. What matters is whether the color and print fit with what you want to represent in the quilt.

Solid Fabrics

This approach is probably most familiar in traditional Amish quilts. Any quilt block will look stunning in solids. It is important to remember that your piecing mistakes will be less forgiving with this fabric set. I used this color set in the Saltbox House quilt. Think, too, of using white as well as black for your background.

Scrap Fabrics

Although this may look like the easiest route, you must approach scrap quilts with a sense of adventure. Working with scraps will force you to grow as a quiltmaker. To work in scrap, you approach each block as an individual unit, not worrying how the previous block looked. The greater the variety of fabrics, the more successful your quilt will be. A comforting way to approach scrap quilts is to work with fabrics you are naturally drawn to. (For another approach, read about the dilemma my students put me in when I made my Postage Stamp quilt.) Most people have developed a fondness for certain color combinations, and those colors resurface again and again. Even though each block is different from the preceding, you will find that a certain color will reappear frequently. If your blocks become disjointed, add more blocks with your comfort color. The reappearance of that color will help tie your blocks together. Working in scrap takes time and patience. It provides a wonderful opportunity to learn the many different qualities of fabric and what happens when they are combined.

Once you have decided on the color set you want to explore, I recommend that you start with at least eighteen different fabrics. While you may find this amount limiting, it will offer you enough variety to start with. There is a good chance that you will add to this collection as your quilt starts to take form. I find that, the more fabric I use in my quilt, the more exciting each piece becomes.

I usually buy third-yard cuts; however, quarter-yard pieces will do if you are on a limited budget. If you buy lots of fabric in small amounts, be willing to help put back the bolts (folded side up, please). This will keep you a welcome customer. You may even discover a wonderful piece that you missed the first time around. Once you have selected your fabrics, put them to the test by making sure they pass in the next three categories. Your reward will be an A+ quilt!

THE TESTS

Light to Dark

All fabrics can be categorized as light, medium, or dark. We usually tend toward the mediums, because they are the "prettiest." It is important to have a balance of all three ranges. If there is not enough light or dark, your quilt will not sparkle. I check this by squinting to see if the light and dark jump out at me. Although this seems like a fairly simple task, it really takes some training. Here is a way to test your skill. Cut several ½" x 6" pieces of fabric and arrange them from light to dark. Attach them to a piece of paper and run it through a black-and-white copy machine. The results may surprise you. Chances are that 80% of your chosen fabric will be in the medium range. Time to rearrange: remove some of the fabrics and get an even balance of light, medium,

Before

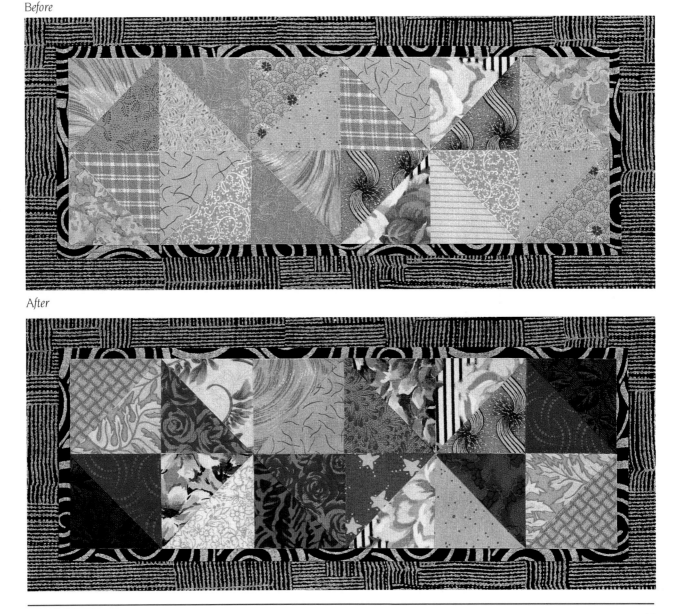

After

and dark. This would be a fun exercise to do with a friend, working from each other's collection. I always keep a watchful eye for light fabrics in each of the color groups, as they are the hardest to find. Although they may not be the pieces that I fall in love with and want to spend money on, they come in handy when it's time to piece quilts!

Character of Print

Character is the size and scale of the print. Like people, each fabric has its own character. How boring if the world were made of the same kind of people. It's the same way with quilts. Make sure the fabrics don't all have the same "look": put in some geometrics, flowers, swirls, stripes, or polka dots. Make sure that these are in all different sizes: we don't all wear the same dress size, either. If you stick to one type of print, your quilt may look like it has chicken pox. Be willing to use those fabrics that Mother wouldn't let you wear. By risking here, a whole new world of fabric selection will open up to you. Squint to make sure the fabrics don't all look the same. If you find that this doesn't help enough, consider buying a reducing glass. A reducing glass is the opposite of a magnifying glass: it brings down the size of the object you are looking at and gives you terrific perspective. Remember: Never eliminate a piece of fabric because you don't like the print; it might be the piece you learn to love the most!

Before

After

Color Groups

Small boxes of crayons, color wheels, and language trick us into thinking that the world is made up of pure colors. When you think of green, a field of grass might come to mind. However, there might be only two bolts of grass green in the quilt store. The base dye color is usually mixed with another color. The green might have a lot of yellow, or possibly blue has been added, changing the look. And this happens with all colors.

I have made several quilts in which I've used every available piece of fabric in a color group, so the quilts don't look as if they came from a kit. In the midst of the quilt, I will find myself running to the quilt store to make sure I haven't left anything out. There's another reason to shop regularly, to keep up your inventory of fabric.

Before

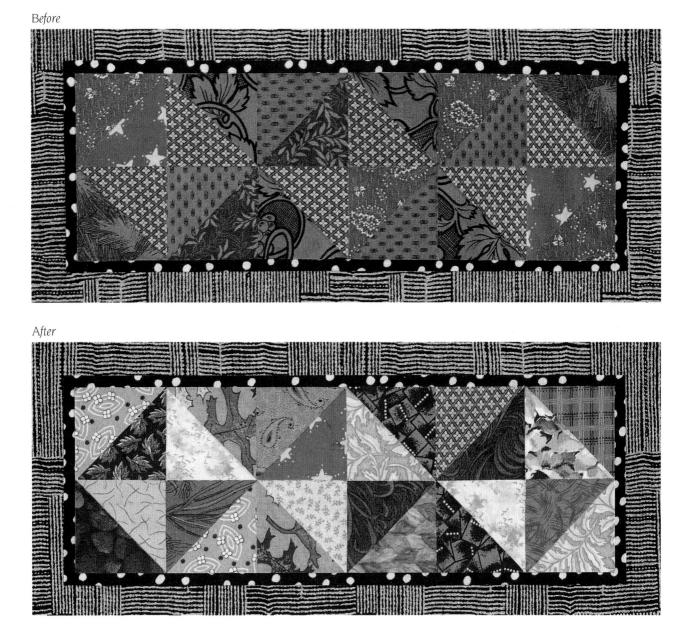

After

FURTHER FABRIC HINTS

Whenever possible, be sure to use at least a touch of white. Often people choose to use either off-white or white prints. If your quilt is predominantly off-white, just a bit of white will add sparkle and crispness. One way to introduce white into the quilt is by using a fabric containing both white and off-white, to act as a bridge. Sometimes it takes just three pieces of white to add light, to make your quilt shine.

Before

After

I *love* stripes and polka dots! Stripes add strength to the other fabrics and complement softer prints. Polka dots are playful, adding whimsy. It's fun to have both appear unexpectedly. Stripes and polka dots are not readily available, so I always watch for them.

Before

After

For variety, use several background fabrics. This can add a lot of interest subtly.

Before

After

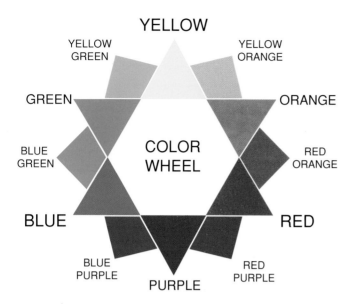

YELLOW

YELLOW GREEN

YELLOW ORANGE

GREEN

ORANGE

BLUE GREEN

COLOR WHEEL

RED ORANGE

BLUE

RED

BLUE PURPLE

RED PURPLE

PURPLE

If you are working primarily with fabrics in one color group, add a touch of its complementary color—the color directly across from it on a standard color wheel. This enriches the basic color set.

Never say there is a fabric you can't work with. All have a place in your quiltmaking, and it's your job to find it. You may just find a new fabric friend. Following my guidelines, you'll be surprised by which fabrics add sparkle and individuality to your quilts.

Before

After

Design

Once you have chosen your blocks and fabrics, you have a few more decisions before you actually cut into your fabric. First is block size. While this might not seem like an important issue, it can make or break your quilt. If your pattern is simple and made from few pieces, I rec-

ommend that you keep the block under 8". If the blocks get too large, you will see sheets of fabric. A good example is the Maple Leaf quilt. Had the blocks been 12", much of the charm would have been lost.

Using the rotary cut-

ting formulas (page 24-25), I calculate the measurements for each segment and piece a few blocks, to see how different manipulations in the following categories can bring life

to my quilt. Remember, I like working with simple blocks, so if a few of them end up on the back of the quilt or in a friendship quilt, it's not the end of the world. Keep in mind that this is a journey without an exact destination.

USING DIFFERENT-SIZED BLOCKS

I love working with blocks that are different sizes—a simple process that produces stunning results. The easi-

est way to use this design technique is to sew units that, when combined, add to the full-size block. It is important to keep the blocks in sizes that work together. For example, the Double Sawtooth Star quilt has 8" and 4" blocks. There were no problems when it came to put

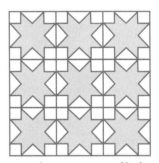

Straight set, same-size blocks

the quilt together. I simply lined the blocks up in horizontal rows, offsetting the vertical rows by putting in the 4" stars. For more complicated combinations with multiple sizes of blocks, you need to approach them like a jigsaw puzzle, piecing different sections at a time.

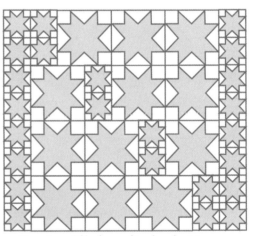

Two sizes of blocks combined and set in rows

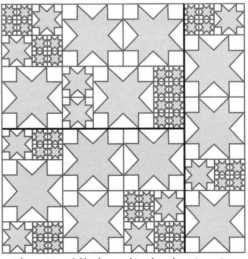

Three sizes of blocks combined and set in units

SECONDARY PATTERNS

When blocks of the same size are set next to each other, wonderful patterns from the negative space in the background can occur. These are called secondary designs. You can check the impact of this by piecing a few of the blocks and putting them together. If time is an issue, you first might want to draw and color a few of your blocks on paper, cut them apart, then arrange them in different sets to see what happens. You may be amazed at the designs that appear. I was pleasantly surprised when I saw all the diamonds appear in the Cherry Basket quilt.

BLOCK ROTATION

A directional block is one that looks different, depending on how it is turned. When you have a directional block, you should consider block rotation. By turning and setting your blocks in an unexpected manner you can make a strong visual statement with even the simplest block. I use this technique often as a fun way to design. If you look at the Maple Leaf quilt, you will see that the blocks have been turned rather randomly. In the Sailboat quilt, the sails face different directions. By changing the direction of the blocks, you give movement to the quilt. I can almost feel the autumn wind whipping the leaves off the trees or picture myself in the middle of a sailboat race.

Before

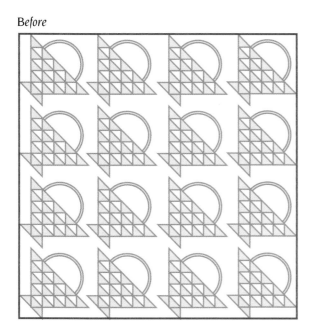

Before

After

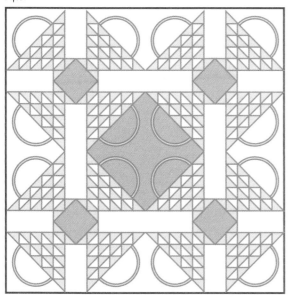

After

BLOCK COMBINATION

I like to use more than one pattern in my quilts. Block combination is useful when your primary block begins to seem boring: try introducing another simple block to complement it, as I did in the Postage Stamp quilt. You can also combine blocks to tell a story, as in the Fishing with Pop-Pop and Sailboat quilts. Combining blocks is an excellent way to spread your wings creatively. You can give very traditional blocks a fresh, unusual look.

BLOCK WITHIN BLOCK

Another successful design technique places a small block within a larger version of the same block. In choosing an appropriate block, look for one that has a large area to accommodate the smaller version, in a manageable size. I have used this trick in the Double Sawtooth Star quilt. I made several 4" stars, then made them the centers of some of the 8" stars. The over-achiever might want to try a triple star, adding a 2" star in the center of the 4" one!

Before

Before

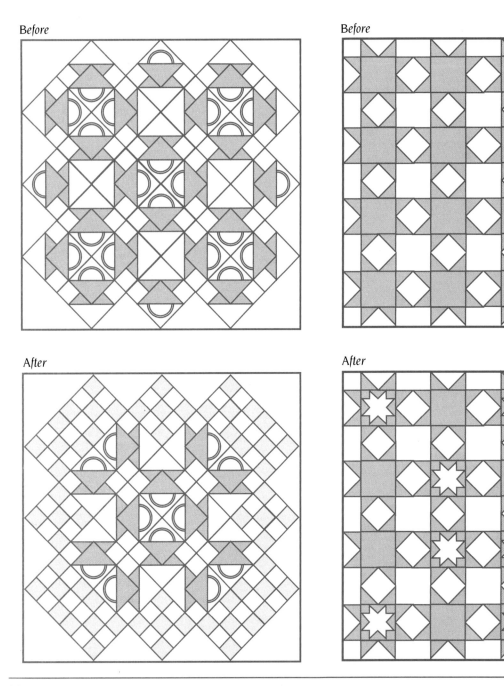

After

After

REPEATING BLOCK PARTS

A block is a combination of shapes, sewn together. Look carefully at the block you have chosen. Learn to identify the different segments of the block. Use your imagination to design your own block by separating and rearranging the basic shapes. For example, the sailboat block has sails made of half-square triangles. Think of all the different things you can do with half-square triangles. When you turn and connect this simple shape, you can make several different blocks such as pinwheels, sawtooth edges, flying geese, or diamonds. In the Sailboat quilt, I decided to use pinwheels around the edge and half-square triangles for water. In the Fishing with

Before

After

Pop-Pop quilt, I devised the tree shape by using the isosceles triangle in a square, as in many star quilts; I then added three rectangles for the trunk.

Use your imagination when you look at your basic block. Remember that a block is just a combination of shapes sewn together. Design your own block by separating and rearranging the shapes. You'll be amazed and delighted by the results.

HUMOR AND SURPRISES

It's fun to put subtle jokes into quilts. This rewards the viewer who takes the time to look closely. Sometimes the surprise can be obvious. In the lake of the Fishing with Pop-Pop quilt you can see the fish that got away. But what is not so obvious is the fabric with buzzing flies and fish lures used in the border. This playing makes quiltmaking a fun journey from beginning to end. It keeps your mind working and gives the quilt a special personality.

LEMONADE

This is a key factor to keep in mind at all times when designing your own quilt: *Often things will not go quite as planned.* Even the best-laid plans can lead you into unexpected challenges. The border may not fit as you intended, the quilt takes on a look you had not expected, or your math work was imprecise. In quiltmaking, too—when life hands you a scrapbag of lemons, make lemonade! When I decided to use pinwheels for the border of my Sailboat quilt, the size went wrong. To correct the problem, I added 1" inner borders on two sides to make the numbers right. And you thought it was a design decision! Some of my favorite quilts have had bumpy journeys.

Laying Out the Quilt

Your work space is as important as the fabric and blocks you have chosen. It is important to have a place to look at your blocks in order to make proper design decisions. I am fortunate to have my own place to work. In fact, when I announced that I was going to set up my sewing room in the living room (After all, just how often did we use it?), it was amazing how quickly my husband removed the bed and dresser from our (former) guest room. My work board is two sheets of ceiling material nailed to the wall, with fleece stapled to it. Small blocks stay up without being pinned. On the wall opposite my work board is a mirror. When I look at my blocks in the mirror, I can get good perspective on my work. If this is an impossible solution for you, hang a piece of fleece on a wall temporarily and pin your blocks to it as they develop. When the day's work is over, you can take it down and re-hang it the next time you work. I strongly recommend a reducing glass, as discussed earlier. I often use both my mirror and a reducing glass. If all else fails, take off your glasses and squint!

I really enjoy this part of the designing process, because it challenges me with decisions. The layout takes time and patience. The results may not be evident immediately, but with a little persistence you too will discover the joys of designing. Here are a few simple guidelines that I always keep in mind and apply when appropriate.

1. Many people think that sashings solve all problems, but often they take away from the integrity of the quilt. It can end up looking like the quiltmaker wanted to have a larger quilt but was too lazy to do the work. Sashings are appropriate only when they are a conscious design decision, made to enhance the look of the quilt. In my Saltbox House quilt the left-hand vertical of the block formed a sashing when connected to the next block. It therefore became necessary to add a horizontal sashing to balance out this vertical unit. So remember to use sashing only if there is a valid reason; otherwise, leave it out.

2. If one block is clearly outstanding, do not put it in the center, but set it off to one side. I like the area near the right or lower right-hand side (that's where artists always sign their work). Notice where the fish that got away and the lighthouse are placed in the Fishing with Pop-Pop and Sailboat quilts. Placing the unusual piece off to one side forces the eye to look at all parts of the quilt.

3. If you use some unusual fabrics that shout, use them sparingly. Place them throughout the surface of the quilt, not just in one area. This makes your eye travel around the entire quilt. This is how I handled the yellow houses in the Saltbox House quilt.

4. If your blocks look very scrappy and disjointed, try putting high-contrast blocks in each corner. This helps to hold the blocks together visually. I used this technique in the Postage Stamp quilt.

5. If you find that your blocks are beginning to overwhelm each other, try putting in some resting blocks—a place for the eyes to re-focus before moving to the next block. In the Sailboat quilt, I used this technique by

adding triangles. Not only did I avoid sashing, but I gave the boats water to sail in.

BORDERS

You must decide how you are going to handle the borders. I never make this decision until my top is complete. If you decide this too soon, you might limit the creative direction your quilt can go.

Inner Border

First, you must consider whether or not it needs an inner border. You might use an inner border to offer some visual relief before adding the final border. This was necessary in the Maple Leaf quilt. Had I sewn the large floral border directly onto the quilt body, the eye would have gotten lost. The inner orange border became an important resting place.

You might use an inner border to hold the quilt blocks together visually. In the Double Sawtooth Star quilt, the sawtooth border was too busy directly next to the pieced surface. The 1" beige inner border held all the blocks together and also gave visual relief. (Notice how the inner border has been pieced of four different fabrics, for added interest.) Sometimes you can use the inner border to repeat a color accent or emphasize a design trick. In the Saltbox House quilt, the inner border was a repeat of the sashing. This added strength and continuity.

Finally, an inner border can also adjust any math errors. As I mentioned before, the 1" inner border on the Sailboat quilt served that purpose. Without it, I would have ended up with half a pinwheel at the top and the bottom. Remember that your inner border can also be a pieced unit. This can be a place to repeat designs, like the diamonds in the Cherry Basket quilt.

After all these considerations, you may decide that your quilt may be perfect as it is and does not need an inner border.

Final Border

Should your final border be pieced or not? In this book, only the Maple Leaf quilt has an unpieced border. It became clear, as the blocks developed, that a pieced border would have been visually too distracting. Generally, however, I like pieced borders because they are one more place to use:

- Repeat block parts—the sawtooth border of the Double Sawtooth Star quilt, the pinwheels of the Sailboat quilt, and the checkerboard of the Saltbox House quilt;

- Block combinations—as in the two basket quilts;
- Humor—Every fisherman dreams of owning a log cabin!

General Instructions

YARDAGE

Quilts for Fabric Lovers celebrates using a variety of fabrics in each quilt. Therefore, the yardage requirements given with the project instructions are the *total* amounts you will need. Fabric stores will often cut a minimum of a quarter-yard, so you may want to buy more than the required total in order to used a wider variety of fabrics. That's OK, because this is a good way to build up your fabric collection. You may also find that you already have some fabrics in your stash that will work well in a project.

PRE-WASHING

Avid fabric lovers manage to collect fabrics in unusual places. Unfortunately, you often don't know the history of the fabric. To check for dangers of shrinkage or dye migration, I strongly recommend pre-washing or testing all fabrics before you put them into your quilt. You can test by cutting a small swatch from the end of the fabric and soaking it for several minutes in a glass of hot water with a swatch of white 100% cotton. If any color appears in the water or on the white swatch, do not use the fabric unless you set the dye permanently. You can soak the suspect piece in white vinegar to set the dye, then re-test; if color still appears in the soak water, do not use the fabric. What is sadder than seeing dye migrating across the surface of a precious quilt?

CUTTING

The cutting numbers given for each project are for *one* block. If I want to cut several pieces of fabric at a time, I stack, press, and cut up to four layers at once. To protect your accuracy, never cut more than four layers together.

PRESSING

The success of your quilt depends upon your care in pressing the blocks. You will see that in each project I indicate the seam allowance directions with arrows. If you follow these pressing directions, your blocks will fit together easily. I choose seam directions for ease of construction, rather than with regard to colors. If you piece carefully, you do not have to worry about pressing dark to light: the light allowance will be against the light fabric. Always press on a firm surface, and avoid pressing bias edges, which may stretch. Press the units right side up to avoid creases in the seam line.

The Finishing Touches

BACKING

Once you've completed your quilt top, it's time to consider the backing. The back can be as interesting as the front, especially when you incorporate some of the same fabrics. No law requires that your quilt back must be made from a single fabric. Extra focus fabric works very well, pieced with some companion fabrics. Any leftover blocks are a delight on the back, and they are a good place for your signature and the date of completion. For the sake of the future generations, always sign and date your quilts, and use only permanent ink. Here are two warnings when you select fabrics for the back.

1. Always use 100% cottons from the quilt shop; *never* use sheets or decorator fabrics, which have a high thread count and are difficult to quilt through. I often take my quilting needle to the store, to make a few test passes through fabric candidates. If the fabric seems to grab or resist the needle, I look for a more workable fabric. This is not a factor if you are machine quilting.

2. If your quilt top is generally light in color, avoid a dark backing fabric; it may show through and dull the effect of the quilt top.

QUILTING

I have two simple philosophies that apply to the quilting of my projects: "Treat the pieced surface as one," and "More is better." How you decide on the quilting, and the amount of quilting, will determine the success of your quilt. I often hang the pieced top on my wall for several days, trying to determine how to handle the surface. Here are a few guidelines that I keep in mind as I ponder.

1. Always approach the pieced top as one unit, never as a set of individual blocks. Many people tend to quilt $\frac{1}{4}$" around the seams. This is how we direct beginners to start, so they don't get bogged down in starting to quilt. Although this is the simplest way to start, I find it unsatisfactory because it pushes all the seam allowances up into your face. Even the simplest grid over the

| Crosshatch | Double crosshatch | Zigzag | Mixed diagonals | Soft curves |

entire surface will provide charming results, as in the Postage Stamp quilt. You might want to try a ¾" repeated soft wave that covers the surface of the quilt, as in the Sailboat quilt, or a combination of both, as in Fishing with Pop-Pop. With an overall pattern, the blocks unite into one quilt. Above are some basic grid ideas that will get you started.

We give so much time to the piecing of our tops that often the quilting becomes secondary. I feel that, whether you are an avid hand quilter or an unapologetic machine quilter, the amount of quilting should never be short-changed. I have traditionally been a hand quilter, but of late I have begun machine quilting. Either way, I treat the pieced surface with respect. Along with a *large* amount of quilting, always fill the surface with an *equal* amount of quilting. If you are using motifs, make sure that they fill the space. This will keep areas from sagging. Keeping these basic rules in mind, I look to quilts of the past for inspiration and design ideas.

BINDING

The final step in constructing the quilt is the binding. Even here, you can be creative. If you look closely at the quilt photographs, you will see that only one does not have a binding pieced from several fabrics. This is another touch that captures the essence of a true fabric lover!

Quick Cutting Magic Numbers

The quilts in this book are based upon blocks built from basic shapes. These shapes have all been rotary cut and have quick-cutting numbers that are constant, no matter how small or how large your block is. If you are unfamiliar with rotary cutting, you should try your wings at this technique. You will find that rotary cutting will save you time, and the results are extremely accurate.

There are two basic rules for finding the numbers for quick cutting.

1. The numbers given will work only with ¼" seam allowances.

2. Measure the finished size of the desired piece and then add the magic number to that size. Do not take into consideration the ¼" seam allowance; the number does that for you.

Squares and Rectangles

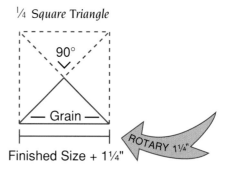

Finished Size + ½"   ROTARY ½"

Triangles: ½ Square Triangle

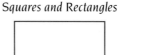
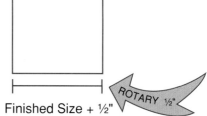

— Grain —

90°   Finished Size + ⅞"   ROTARY ⅞"

Cut a square at the finished size + ⅞" then cut ◨ .

¼ Square Triangle

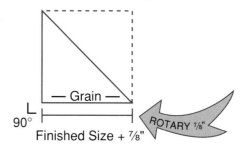

90°

— Grain —

Finished Size + 1¼"   ROTARY 1¼"

Cut a square at the finished size + 1¼" then cut ⊠ .

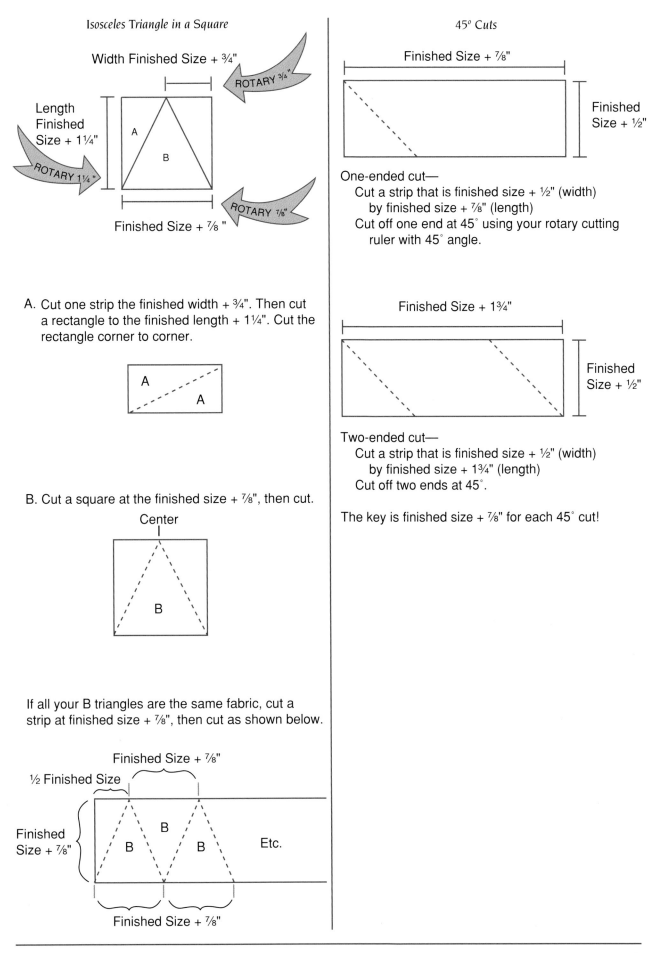

Isosceles Triangle in a Square

Width Finished Size + ¾"

ROTARY ¾"

Length Finished Size + 1¼"

ROTARY 1¼"

A

B

ROTARY ⅞"

Finished Size + ⅞"

A. Cut one strip the finished width + ¾". Then cut a rectangle to the finished length + 1¼". Cut the rectangle corner to corner.

A

A

B. Cut a square at the finished size + ⅞", then cut.

Center

B

If all your B triangles are the same fabric, cut a strip at finished size + ⅞", then cut as shown below.

Finished Size + ⅞"

½ Finished Size

Finished Size + ⅞"

B

B   B

Etc.

Finished Size + ⅞"

45° Cuts

Finished Size + ⅞"

Finished Size + ½"

One-ended cut—
Cut a strip that is finished size + ½" (width) by finished size + ⅞" (length)
Cut off one end at 45° using your rotary cutting ruler with 45° angle.

Finished Size + 1¾"

Finished Size + ½"

Two-ended cut—
Cut a strip that is finished size + ½" (width) by finished size + 1¾" (length)
Cut off two ends at 45°.

The key is finished size + ⅞" for each 45° cut!

MAPLE LEAF

This quilt is 68" x 68" and contains sixty-one 6" blocks.
Skill Level: Beginning

During a lecture to a quilt guild, I related an incident from my student days at San Francisco State University. I had been whining about the use of a certain color. The teacher stopped the class, pointed her finger at me, and said, "To say you hate a color tells me you are ignorant of its use!" The impact of that statement has changed my artistic life: thank you, Marika Contompasis. As my lecture to the guild continued, I commented on my dislike of the maple leaf block. Lecture ended, meeting proceeded, and guess what the block of the month was! I was reminded that every bolt of fabric—and every block pattern—has a place in this world. Thanks to the quiltmakers of Modesto, California, for laughing at my embarrassment: this quilt is dedicated to you!

The maple leaf block is easy to construct: it does not have many pieces. When using a simple pattern, I like to keep the block small. Large units of fabric can become overpowering. In this instance, I chose to make my maple leaf 6". *Key:* If a block gets too big, the large planes of fabric make the block look clunky.

The focus fabric that I chose was fun to work with, because there were so many different colors in it. At first glance you see green, red, yellow, black, and orange. More important, there are many different greens, reds, yellows, and oranges. I found myself using fabrics that were not necessarily my favorites; without them, the quilt would have been monotonous. *Key:* Be willing to use fabrics that might not be your favorites.

The background is made from nine unusual black fabrics. I looked for fabrics that had different character. If you look closely, you will find different sizes and styles of dots, large swirls, checks, grids and an overall lizard print. This is much more interesting than a background of solid black. *Key:* Look for fabrics that have different size and scale prints.

The maple leaf block has direction to it, meaning that it looks different when turned in all directions. Rather than having all the blocks set one way, I turned them and set the blocks on point to get a swirling effect. You can almost feel the wind whipping the leaves off the trees on a brisk autumn day. *Key:* If your block has

direction, try rotating it for an unusual effect.

Fabric Requirements

The following fabric requirements are the *total* amount of yardage needed to complete your quilt. See General Instructions: Yardage, page 23. The greater the variety of fabrics you use in your quilt, the more interesting it will be.

Large-print focus fabric: 2 yards
Black background: 2 yards
Maple leaves: 2¼ yards
Inner striped border: ½ yard
Backing: 4 yards

6" Maple Leaf

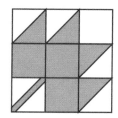

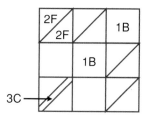

CUTTING

The following numbers are for *one* maple leaf. (See General Instructions: Cutting, page 23.)

Traditional: Use template patterns 1B, 2F, 3C.

MAPLE LEAF

(1B) Cut three 2½" squares.

(2F) Cut two 2⅞" squares, then cut ◩.

(3C) Cut one ¾" x 3½" rectangle.

BACKGROUND

(2F) Cut three 2⅞" squares, then cut ◩.

(1B) Cut one 2½" square.

PIECING AND PRESSING

(The arrows indicate which way to press.)

For the stem, piece background 2F to each side of 3C and trim to 2½" square.

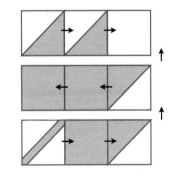

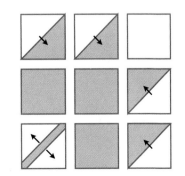

Setting

Hint: This quilt is set on point, so it requires half-square and quarter-square triangles of the focus fabric to complete the top. After you make your blocks and are about to cut the triangles for the sides, I recommend that you first cut and set aside the fabric for the border from the length of the yardage so that you won't later have to piece it. Be generous in the length of this cut; you can trim it to the exact size later.

Outer border

Cut two $7\frac{1}{2}$" x $54\frac{1}{2}$" border strips.

Cut two $7\frac{1}{2}$" x $68\frac{1}{2}$" border strips.

Inner border

Cut 2" wide inner border. (See step 3.)

Side quarter-square triangles

Cut five $9\frac{3}{4}$" squares, then cut ⊠. (No template pattern given.)

Corner triangles

Cut two $5\frac{1}{8}$" squares, then cut ◹. (No template pattern given.)

1. Lay out your blocks as shown. Note that they are set on point, and the blocks are rotated for a whirlwind effect.
2. Join the pieced blocks and the side and corner triangles in a diagonal set.
3. The inner border has been pieced to get the desired length. Try to hide the piecing within the striped print. Note that the lower right-hand inner border has nine cut and pieced rotated squares of the striped fabric. (This creates an added surprise.) Sew on the inner border.
4. Sew on the outer floral border.

Congratulations! Your maple leaf quilt is now ready to layer, baste, and quilt.

Maple Leaf
Machine quilted by Alex Anderson

POSTAGE STAMP

This quilt is 57½" x 57½". It contains one hundred and thirteen 4½"
postage stamp baskets and thirty-two 4½" nine-patches.
Skill level: Beginning

I have learned in the course of teaching that my greatest teachers have been my students. Whenever I teach, I encourage my students to stretch their creativity by working with fabrics that they might not be comfortable with. I always assure them there is *nothing* that can't go together.

In preparing for a workshop on baskets, I decided to brush up on the art of basket-making and piece a few of these 4½" baskets. Minutes turned into hours as I found myself becoming addicted to the process of choosing fabrics and piecing the little units together. I could see that my first scrap quilt was beginning to take form. When some students got wind of this project, they decided to add to the challenge by graciously giving me lime green, red cow, pumpkin, and Indian fabrics! After all, they reminded me, there isn't any fabric combination that can't work. Those fabrics are all in this quilt!

 Notice that the inner blocks are lighter than the outer blocks. This draws your eye to the center of the quilt, providing a focal point. The blocks are set on point and rotated to echo the 1978 postage stamp. While I was arranging the blocks on my design wall, my son commented that the quilt looked "old." The pink and brown nine-patch gives the quilt a nineteenth-century look.

When you are working with a scrap quilt, here are a few guidelines that will help make the journey less bumpy.

Key 1: Keep the block size small. That is why I decided to work with a 4½" basket. If the blocks get too large, the unusual fabrics become overwhelming and take over the quilt.

Key 2: Have a space where you can lay out the blocks and look at them. After you have made three-quarters of the blocks, you might find that certain colors need to be added for your personal comfort. I found blue and brown gave me solace.

Key 3: When your blocks are finished, try putting high-contrast blocks in the corners to help hold the quilt together. I chose to do this with the baskets and not with the nine-patch, because the nine-patch acts as the border that frames the set.

Key 4: Note that within the pink and brown nine-patch border there is one blue and brown nine-patch. A hundred years from now, a great story will be fabricated about this block—perhaps that the little old lady who made the quilt ran out of pink and had to substitute blue due to hard times. Let's leave it to the historians to keep up the great stories!

Fabric Requirements

This is a scrap quilt and is ideal for a friendship group or class project. Each participant can cut and share from her own collection.

Baskets: Each basket requires two pieces of fabric, each measuring 4½" x 6½". There is a total of two-hundred and twenty-six pieces this size. If your stash of fabric doesn't support this project, it would be fun to exchange fabric with friends. Of course, this is the perfect time to beef up your own collection at your local quilt store! The simplicity of this block offers a terrific chance to explore any fabric collection you might want to work with.

Postage Stamp
Machine quilted by Alex Anderson

The following fabric require- ments are the total amount of yardage needed to make the nine- patches. See General Instructions: Yardage, page 23. I found my fabric collection lacking in pinks and took this opportunity to stock it up. The nine-patches would work quite nicely from just two fabrics, too.

Pink: ⅝ yard

Brown: ⅝ yard

Brown setting triangles: ½ yard

Backing: 3½ yards

4½" Postage Stamp Basket

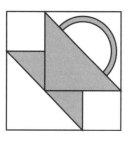

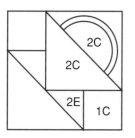

The following cutting numbers are for *one* postage stamp basket. (See General Instructions: Cutting, page 23.)

CUTTING

Traditional: Use template patterns 1C, 2C, 2E.

BASKET

(2C) Cut one 3⅞" square, then cut ◩. (Save the other half-square triangle for the bias handle.)

(2E) Cut one 2⅜" square, then cut ◩.

Handle: Cut a 1" strip off the bias edge of the extra triangle. Press in half lengthwise. Note that the ends of the bias handle are not even.

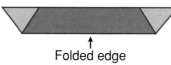

Folded edge

BACKGROUND

(2C) Cut one 3⅞" square, then cut ◩.

Staystitch one of the triangles ⅛" in on the bias edge. This will keep it from stretching when you sew on the handle.

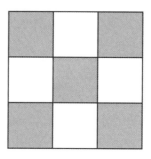

(1C) Cut two 2" squares.

PIECING AND PRESSING

Use pattern 2C for handle placement. Trace onto your fabric with a removable marking tool. (Always test your tool on a scrap of the fabric to make sure the mark comes out.) I use a removable marking pencil.

Hand or machine appliqué the bias handle onto the staystitched background piece 2C. *Caution*: Match the right side of the back- ground fabric to the longest right side of the bias handle, folded edge to the inside. Flip the handle up over the stitched edge and whipstitch down the outside finished edge.

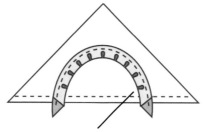

Folded edge

The arrows indicate which way to press.

The ^ indicates which edge or point to line up.

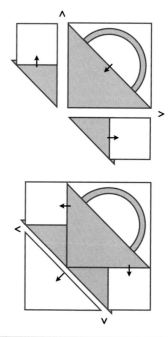

4½" Nine-patch

1C PINK	1C BROWN	PINK
BROWN	PINK	BROWN
PINK	BROWN	PINK

The following instructions are for one nine-patch. (See General Instructions: Cutting, page 23.) If you are not conservative with your fabric, cut off 2" strips from each piece, then cut off your squares as needed. This wastes fabric but will save time.

CUTTING

Traditional: Use template
pattern 1C.

Pink: Cut five 2" squares.

Brown: Cut four 2" squares.

PIECING AND PRESSING

(The arrows indicate which way
to press.)

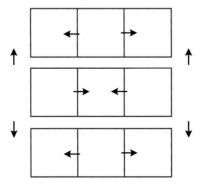

SIDE QUARTER-SQUARE TRIANGLES

(No template pattern given.)
Cut eight 7 ⅝" squares, then
cut ⊠ .

CORNER TRIANGLES

(No template pattern given.)
Cut two 4⅛" squares, then
cut ◩ .

1. Lay out your blocks as shown.
2. Join the pieced blocks with the
   side and corner triangles in a
   diagonal set.

You did it! Your late 1800's
basket quilt is now ready to layer,
baste, and quilt.

DOUBLE SAWTOOTH STAR

This quilt is 50" x 54" and contains twenty-five
8" double sawtooth stars and thirty-two 4" sawtooth stars.
Skill Level: Beginning/Intermediate

The sawtooth star has always been one of my favorite blocks—so simple looking, yet it always makes stunning quilts. Early in my quiltmaking career, I had a one-woman show at Empty Spools in Alamo, California, a quilt store where I taught. One quilt in particular caught co-owner Diana McClun's eye and, much to my surprise, she wanted it for the first book she was writing with Laura Nownes, *Quilts! Quilts!! Quilts!!!* I couldn't believe my quilt was going to be in a book! At the time, I was struggling to be a "contemporary artist/quiltmaker," searching for an individual style. It never occurred to me that a simple sawtooth star quilt could be appropriate for public exposure. I learned two valuable lessons from that invitation: while I enjoy working with classic quilt blocks, the fact they are made today makes them contemporary; never underestimate the impact of a quilt you make. Whether it is your first endeavor, a child's doll quilt held together with six ties, or a six-thousand-hour Baltimore Album quilt, they all come from the same place—your heart. Each quilt needs to be treasured and respected.

This quilt was fun to make because I chose to work with a focus fabric that had colors I rarely work with, purple and pink. It is the darkest background in two of the 8" stars. Finds like this present one more reason to visit the local quilt shops frequently. I used this fabric because of the variety of colors in it. When you use a focus fabric, it is important to remember that it need not be repeated many times in your quilt. It is a fabric color reference, that's all. This quilt would have been much darker-looking if I had kept the background fabrics as deep as the focus fabric. That is why I used several off-white-on-beige and white-on-white prints. *Key:* For a crisp-looking quilt, add white; sometimes you need just a touch to do the trick. Notice how some of the smaller stars have colored backgrounds. This gives the quilt depth.

This quilt is made up of blocks of two different sizes. With the exception of the top and bottom row, each row has two 4" stars breaking the unity of the 8" blocks. It looks complicated at first glance, but it is easy to put together if you approach one row at a time. This is one of my favorite sets, because you can use it for so many different types of blocks. It works every time. *Key:* The easiest way to work in multi-sized blocks is to work with two sizes. When using several sizes, make sure that the block sizes divide evenly into each other. For ease of set, piece them together into large blocks that will work together in the final set.

Before I added the sawtooth border, I decided to put an inner border to help give the eye a resting spot. Rather than using just one fabric, I used four striped fabrics. The lighter stripes are on the top, working to the darker at the bottom. Notice how I slipped in a little bit of polka dot on the lower right-hand side for added interest. *Key:* It adds interest whenever you use a broad variety of fabrics. People expect to see one set of choices; surprise them with more!

Fabric Requirements

The following fabric requirements are the *total* amount of yardage needed to complete your quilt. See General Instructions:

Double Sawtooth Star
Machine quilted by Alex Anderson

Yardage, page 23.
  Stars: 2½ yards
  Background: 2¼ yards
  Inner border: ¼ yard
  Backing: 3¼ yards

4" Sawtooth Star

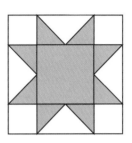

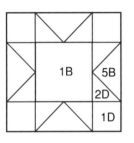

The following cutting numbers are for *one* sawtooth star. (See General Instructions: Cutting, page 23.)

CUTTING

Traditional: Use template patterns 1B, 1D, 2D, 5B.

STAR

(1B) Cut one 2½" square.

(2D) Cut four 1⅞" squares, then cut ◨.

BACKGROUND

(5B) Cut one 3¼" square, then cut ⊠.

(1D) Cut four 1½" squares.

PIECING AND PRESSING

The arrows indicate which way to press.

The ^ indicates which edge or point to line up.

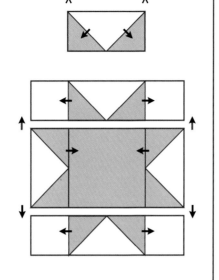

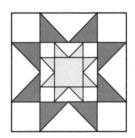

8" Double Sawtooth Star

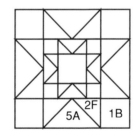

The following cutting numbers are for *one* double sawtooth star.

Cut and piece the 4" inner star as before.

CUTTING

Traditional: Use template patterns 1B, 2F, 5A.

STAR

(2F) Cut four 2⅞" squares, then cut ◨.

BACKGROUND

(5A) Cut one 5¼" square, then cut ⊠.

(1B) Cut four 2½" squares.

PIECING AND PRESSING

The arrows indicate which way to press.

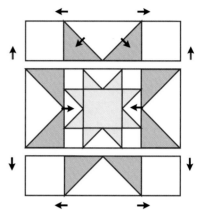

Inner Border

Cut at least 200" of 1½"-wide sashing. Piece as needed.

Border

The border is made up of one hundred ninety-two 2" half-square triangles pieced from the various colored and beige-white fabrics.

Traditional: Use template patterns 1B, 2F.

Cut forty-eight 2⅞" squares of colored prints, then cut ◨.

Cut forty-eight 2⅞" squares of various beige-white prints, then cut ◨.

Cut four 2½" squares for corner blocks.

Piece the half-square triangles together, press to dark, and arrange as shown. Note how the triangles change direction at random. This is an unusual way to handle the turning of the corners. Before sewing your triangles into rows, try arranging them in a different order. You might be pleasantly surprised at your results.

Setting

1. Arrange your blocks as shown.
2. Join your blocks in a straight set.
3. Sew on the inner border.
4. Sew on the pieced outer border.
   You did it! Your quilt is now ready to layer, baste, and quilt.

SALTBOX HOUSE

The quilt is 55" x 62". It contains forty-nine 6" saltbox houses and a 1" checkerboard border.
Skill Level: Beginning/Intermediate

I have always wanted to make a house quilt. Periodically, I would browse through my quilt books and magazines for ideas. Soon, I would change my mind because of the complexity of the houses. One day this little saltbox house pattern fell into my hands. Not only did this house have character, but it looked easy! About the same time, our family was facing the dreaded task of relocating, forcing me to leave behind the house of my dreams. As we started to search for our new home, each house started to look like the last. I remembered simpler days. In the middle of the trauma of moving came the inspiration for my quilt—rows of endless houses pieced in Amish colors! This is the first quilt pieced in my new workroom, and the unexpected joy of the move is reflected in the exciting checkerboard border.

I love working with the jewel tones that are so beautifully used in Amish quilts. When working with these colors I have found the trick is to introduce some light pastels and yellow. These fabrics will make your quilt glow. *Key:* When working with a black background, be sure to include some very light colors.

After all my little houses were pieced, I noticed that the left-hand side of the block formed a vertical sashing. In order to get balance, I had to add horizontal sashing. All of the cornerstones of the sashing could have been red, but different colors add interest. *Key:* When you add some unexpected colors, be sure to carry them throughout the quilt so that the eye moves from one edge to the other.

My new quilting neighbor, Joyce Moss, suggested a checkerboard border to repeat a block segment. It was so much fun to piece the segments of color and pin them to the wall around the quilt. When it came time to piece the border onto the top, the checkerboard wouldn't check! I couldn't believe it. Rather than agonize over the situation, I introduced the three strips of black fabric, calling it a design decision. *Key:* Many times in creative quiltmaking you will be handed lemons: enjoy the lemonade.

Fabric Requirements

The following fabric requirements are the *total* amount of yardage needed to complete your quilt. See General Instructions:

Yardage, page 23.
   Houses: 1⅝ yards
   Black background: 3 yards
   Border: These are the colors I chose to use. You may want to wait to buy these after you piece the top. You can then make changes that are pleasing to your eye.
   Yellow: ¼ yard
   Orange: ¼ yard
   Fuchsia: ¼ yard
   Red: ⅓ yard (includes cornerstones)
   Purple: ¼ yard
   Blue: ¼ yard
   Green: ¼ yard
   Backing: 3¾ yards

6" Saltbox House

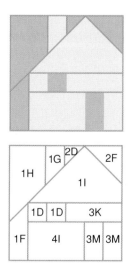

The following cutting numbers are for *one* saltbox house block. (See General Instructions: Cutting, page 23.)

CUTTING

Traditional: Use template patterns 1D, 1F, 1G, 1H, 1I, 2D, 2F, 3K, 3M, 4I.

Saltbox House

(1I) Cut one 7¼" square, then cut ⊠. Then measure 1⅜" from the right-hand bottom base and cut off. (You will get four rooftops from this.)

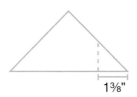

1⅜"

(1G) Cut one 2⅞ x 1½" rectangle. Then cut off the right-hand end at 45°.

(1D) Cut one 1½" square.
(3K) Cut one 1½" x 3½" rectangle.
(3M) Cut one 1½" x 2½" rectangle.
(4I) Cut one 2½" x 3½" rectangle.

Background

(These are cutting numbers for the forty-nine houses.)
(1H) Cut forty-nine 2½" x 4⅞" rectangles. Then cut off one end of each at 45°.

(2D) Cut twenty-five 1⅞" squares, then cut ◨.
(2F) Cut twenty-five 2⅞" squares, then cut ◨.
(1D) Cut forty-nine 1½" squares.
(3M) Cut forty-nine 1½" x 2½" rectangles.
(1F) Cut forty-nine 1½" x 3⅞" rectangles, then cut off one end of each at 45°.

PIECING AND PRESSING

The arrows indicate which way to press.
The ^ indicates which edge or point to line up.

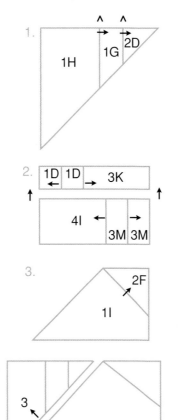

CUTTING

Sashing

Traditional: Use template patterns 1D, 3G, 3H.
(3H) Cut fifty-six 1½" x 5½" black rectangles for the horizontal sashing.
(3G) Cut seven 1½" x 6½" black rectangles for the right-hand vertical sashing.
(1D) Cut sixty-four 1½" red squares for the cornerstones.

Border

Cut twenty-seven to thirty 1½" x 42" crosswise strips of black fabric.
Cut six to nine 1½" x 42" crosswise strips of each color.
1. Lay out the house blocks and sashing as shown.
2. Join the pieced blocks and sashing in a straight set.
3. Sew the checkerboard border by strip piecing.

Strip Piecing

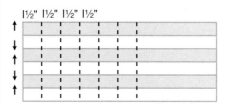

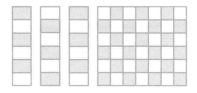

1. Sew three black and three same-colored strips together, alternating colors (for example: black, yellow, black, yellow, black, yellow).
2. Press to black.
3. Cut the pieced strips into 1½"-wide units.

4. Flip and sew to get the checker-board look.
5. Arrange the border as shown. Note that three strips of black

have been introduced into the border in order to make the checkerboard work!
6. Sew on the pieced border.

Great! Your house quilt is now ready to layer, baste, and quilt, to snuggle under on a cold winter night.

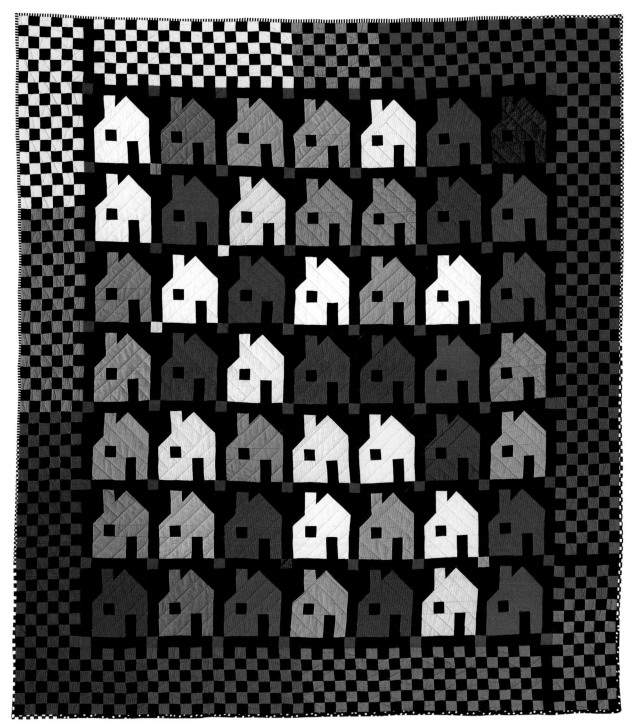

Saltbox House
Machine quilted by Alex Anderson

FISHING WITH POP-POP

The quilt is 48" x 48". It contains three different blocks and appliqué.
Skill Level: Intermediate

- Thirty-eight 4" x 6" pine trees
- Twenty-eight 6" x 6" log cabins
- Ninety-six 2" half-square triangle units

Fishing has never been a sport that I've invested my time in. You can imagine Grandpa's delight when Joey was born: his fishing partner had arrived at last! When Joey was small, he caught a fish with a hook and string. Now, under the skill and guidance of Grandpa, Joey has learned the finer techniques of fishing. Either person has only to say, "Want to go fishing?," and they are off. The best part of Joey's fishing career has been his ability to out-catch Grandpa. This quilt commemorates the time that Joey caught many, and Grandpa none.

Choosing the fabric for this quilt was fun. I tried to incorporate fabrics with prints that related to the themes of the units. For example, several of the trees have a leafy print, and some of the tree trunks look like bark. *Key:* When

piecing a block with a theme, look for fabrics that have related images. If the subject matter isn't available, however, don't drive yourself crazy searching. Notice that there are several different greens in this quilt: not all the trees came from the same dye lot! *Key:* Be willing to use fabrics that may not have the exact color you have chosen. This adds interest.

This is a story quilt simply constructed from three different blocks. By repeating a simple tree block, you can create a forest, and the blue half-square triangles form a pond. The pieced fish in the pond was created by rotating six yellow half-square triangles. *Key:* Work with blocks that have a common multiple, so that setting them together will not be a problem.

I achieved an interesting zigzag border by rotating a log cabin block. You can create different looks by using unusual colors or by setting your blocks in a unique direction. Possibly your fisherman catches only at dusk: you might then want to use darker sky fabric for an evening mood. Use the blocks and fabric to tell your story. *Key:* Use a design board or piece of fleece pinned to the wall to work

out your story.

Often a quilt is made more interesting by adding appliqué. This quilt would have been fine without the string of fish, but they do add playfulness. People limit themselves by avoiding appliqué at all costs. It really takes little effort and produces fabulous results. Keep yourself open to all aspects of quiltmaking. This is how we continue to grow as quiltmakers.

Fabric Requirements

The following fabric requirements are the *total* amount of yardage needed to complete your quilt. See General Instructions: Yardage, page 23. The greater the variety of fabrics you use in your quilt, the more interesting it will be. Half the fun of making this quilt is looking for unusual prints of foliage, tree bark, and water. I hit the jackpot when I found fabric with fish lures and buzzing flies! These little details really count.

Brown: 1 yard
Green: 1¼ yard
Beige-white: 2 yards
Blue: ¼ yard
Yellow: ¼ yard
Red: ⅛ yard

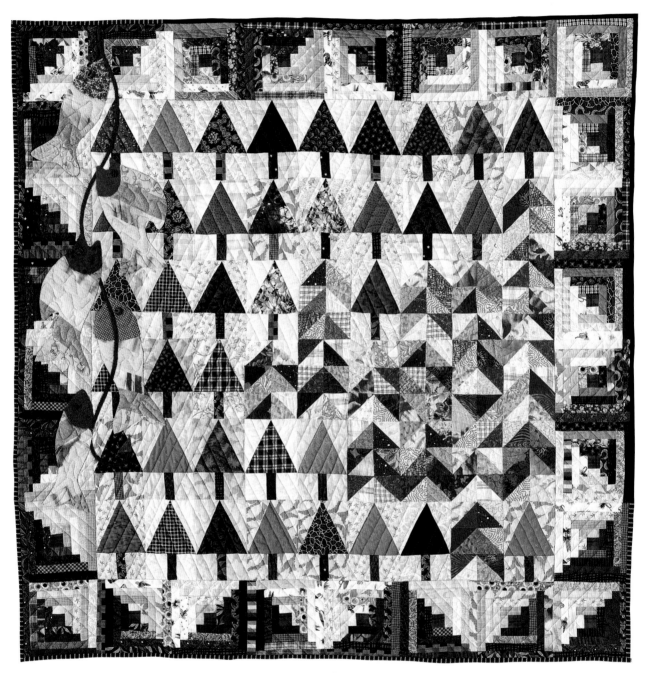

Fishing with Pop-Pop
Machine quilted by Alex Anderson

Blue: ⅛ yard, or 1 yard of double-fold bias ¼" wide, for fishing line
Backing: 3 yards

4" x 6" Pine Tree

The following cutting numbers are for *one* pine tree block. (See General Instructions: Cutting, page 23.)

CUTTING

Traditional: Use template patterns 4J, 4K, 5F, 5G.

Pine tree

(5G) Cut one 4⅞" square, then cut as shown. (This cut produces a lot of waste. If fabric conservation is important, trace pattern 5G.)

(4K) Cut one 1¼" by 2½" rectangle.

Background

(5F) Cut a strip 2¾" by at least 10½". Fold and press end to end, right sides together. Cut the rectangle a perfect 2¾" x 5¼". Then cut on the diagonal as shown. (This will give you an extra set for another tree.)

(4J) Cut two 2⅛" x 2½" rectangles.

PIECING AND PRESSING

The arrows indicate which way to press.

The ^ indicates which edge or point to line up.

6" Log Cabin

Log cabins are fun to mass produce. So, rather than cutting each log individually, I cut several strips of beige fabric and several strips of the green and brown fabrics. Then I pick them up randomly out of the light or appropriate dark pile as needed. If you want to copy this quilt as shown, you will need eleven green and seventeen brown log cabins.

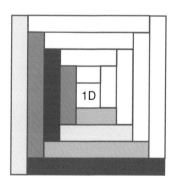

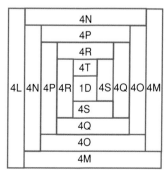

CUTTING

Traditional: Use template patterns 1D, 4L through 4T for logs.

Red Center

(1D) Cut twenty-eight 1½" squares.

Light and Dark Logs

Cut several 1⅛" strips:
Beige-white totaling 1 yard
Green totaling ½ yard
Brown totaling ¾ yard

PIECING AND PRESSING

The arrows indicate which way to press.

Keep adding clockwise and pressing out until your cabin is completed.

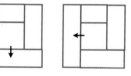

Water and the Fish in Water: 2" half-square triangles

Traditional: Use template pattern 2F.

Separate your blue fabric into light and dark piles.
Dark blue
Cut forty-eight 2⅞" squares, then cut ◨.
Light blue
Cut forty-eight 2⅞" squares, then cut ◨.

(Note that, for some of the light blue water, I used beige to help blend into the tree background.)

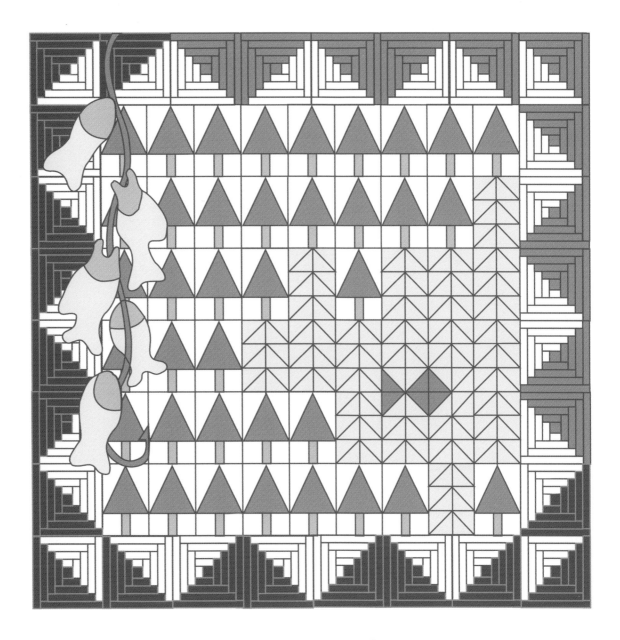

FISH IN WATER

Cut three 2⅞" squares of yellow, then cut ◨ .

Piecing and Pressing

Sew the light blue triangles to the dark blue triangles and press to the darker. Make ninety half-square triangle units. When you get to the fish area, make the six yellow/blue half-square triangle units.

1. Lay out your blocks as shown.
2. Join the blocks together in a straight set.

FISH LINE

1. The fish line is ½" wide. (You can buy double-fold bias ¼" wide.)

You will need at least 1 yard of line. To make your own line, use a ¼" bias bar. Cut a 1" strip on the bias. Fold and sew a ¼" seam allowance. Using the bias bar, press the seams to one side.

2. Pin the line in place on the top, remembering the appliquéd fish hook at the end of the line. (Use the hook pattern on page 63.)

FISH

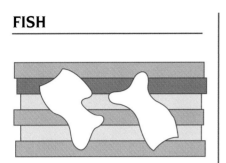

1. Cut strips of yellow fabric 1½" to 2" wide and sew them together, making your own pieced fabric.
2. Cut the fish bodies from freezer paper and align and press them to the right side of the fabric. Cut out the fish, adding ¼" around the edges. (Use the fish patterns on page 63.)
3. Cut the fish heads from freezer paper and align and press them to the right side of the fabric. Cut out the heads, adding ¼" around the edges.
4. Use thread color to match the fish and line.
5. Arrange, pin, and appliqué the fish and heads into place. Turn the edges of the fabric under, keeping it smooth and nicely shaped.
6. Appliqué the fish eyes, using the same technique as above.

Now that your top is complete, you are ready to layer, baste, and quilt as you dream of your vacation at the lake!

SAILBOAT

This quilt is 44" x 48" and contains a combination of different blocks.
Skill Level: Intermediate

- One 10" x 14" lighthouse
- Eight 4" sawtooth stars
- Forty-one 4" pinwheels
- Forty-nine 2" half-square triangle units
- Twelve sailboats of various sizes with 2" half-square triangles for sails

As a child, I was taught many survival skills in the six-foot sailboat Dad built. Being shown the basics of rowing and deposited in the middle of a lake taught me to stick with things until the end. Dad turned 70 in the summer of 1993. He decided to sponsor the First Annual Joey Sladky 70th Birthday Family Reunion on the shores of Rowley's Bay, Door County, Wisconsin. Of course, a quilt was the perfect gift, and so came the Sailboat quilt. I designed this quilt one block at a time. Each boat began to take on a life of its own. Soon a regatta began to form, like the ones that taught me a quiltmaking lesson: When presented with unfamiliar fabrics or patterns, I stick to the project until a "shore line" is in sight.

When you choose to combine different block patterns, you can achieve a story quilt with very little effort. I find it very satisfying to work one block at a time, developing the course of the quilt as it takes form. *Key:* When using this technique, remember to keep the block sizes in multiples of each other (such as 2", 4", 8") for ease of set. For added interest I have offset the blocks with 2" half-square triangles. *Key:* Small, simple pieced units that offset blocks give quilts a more complex look.

I decided to work with a patriotic theme, perfect for a July birthday. Once I decide on a color set, the fabric variety is endless. *Key:* If your color set is a theme that viewers will be familiar with, you can become very creative with your fabric combinations. They *will* go together in the end. You can also hunt out appropriate prints: it was particularly fun to include sea shell, lighthouse, and star fabrics, to give the quilt a playful pictorial mood.

Surprises are always fun to find in quilts. Notice how, in the border, a beige star has been added, and there is one red star in the body of the quilt. An A+ quilt takes more than one minute to view. *Key:* Whenever possible, add a few hidden surprises to make the quilt more interesting.

Fabric Requirements

The following fabric requirements are the *total* amount of yardage needed to complete your quilt. (See General Instructions: Yardage, page 23.) The greater the variety of fabrics you use in your quilt, the more interesting it will be. If you find that the dark blue background disturbs you where the stars don't match up in the lighthouse block, choose a smaller-scale star print. I do prefer the folk-art look of mismatched prints, especially in scrap-type quilts.

Red: 1¼ yard
Blue: 2 yards
White-beige: 1¼ yard
Fabric for the lighthouse is included in the beige yardage. If you are lucky enough to find a novelty fabric for the lighthouse, you will need a piece that is at least 4" x 12".

Backing: 3 yards

Sailboat
Machine quilted by Alex Anderson

Sailboats

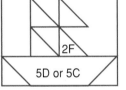

CUTTING

This quilt is made up of sailboats of several different sizes. Each sailboat has either a 2" x 8" or a 2" x 10" finished hull. Each sail is constructed with 2" finished half-square triangles. The background is filled with 2"-wide finishing strips.

The following numbers are for the different parts needed to construct a sailboat. I suggest that you first cut the red hull, then design the sail by laying out the half-square triangles. When you find a pleasing arrangement, put in the background. You might enjoy designing your own regatta. If you design your own boats, the set will be different from the set shown. But they will all fit together, because they are constructed in units of 2" multiples.

See General Instructions: Cutting, page 23.

Traditional: Use template patterns 2F, 5C, 5D.

(5D) 8" Hull: Cut one 9¼" x 2½" strip, then cut off each end at 45°.

(5C) 10" Hull: Cut one 11¼" x 2½" strip, then cut off each end at 45°.

(2F) Sails: Cut the desired number of blue and white 2⅞" squares, then cut ◩. Cut one extra blue square for the base of the boat. (Remember that each square will make two triangles.)

Background: Cut a 2½" strip the desired length plus ½". (No template pattern given.)

PIECING AND PRESSING

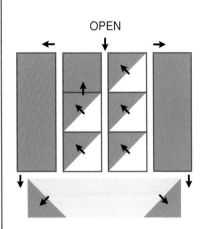

OPEN

1. Press light to dark.
2. Sew the background triangles onto the hull.
3. Sew the triangles together for the sail.
4. Construct the background and sail together in rows.
5. Sew the rows together.
6. Sew the sail unit to the hull unit.

4" Sawtooth Star

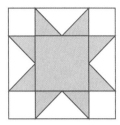

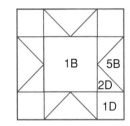

CUTTING

The following cutting numbers are for *one* star. (See General Instructions: Cutting, page 23.)

Traditional: Use template patterns 1B, 1D, 2D, 5B.

Star

(1B) Cut one 2½" square.

(2D) Cut four 1⅞" squares, then cut ◩.

Background

(5B) Cut one 3¼" square, then cut ⊠.

(1D) Cut four 1½" squares.

PIECING AND PRESSING

The arrows indicate which way to press.

The ^ indicates which edge or point to line up.

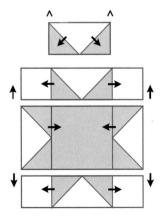

4" Pinwheels and 2" Half-Square Triangles

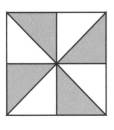

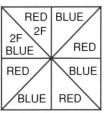

CUTTING

The following cutting numbers are for *one* pinwheel. See General Instructions: Cutting, page 23.

Traditional: Use template pattern 2F.

Red

(2F) Cut two 2⅞" squares, then cut ◪.

Blue

(2F) Cut two 2⅞" squares, then cut ◪.

PIECING AND PRESSING

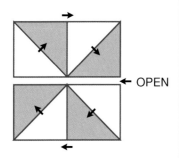

For half-square triangles, use the same cutting numbers as for the pinwheels. Press to the darker fabric.

Lighthouse

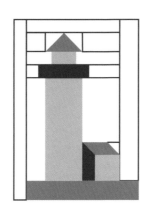

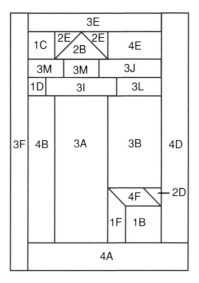

CUTTING

The following cutting numbers are for the lighthouse. There are many pieces in this lighthouse block. I suggest that, as you cut each piece, you arrange them on a table in correct order so you won't get confused. Despite the many pieces, construction is fairly straight-forward.

Traditional: Use template patterns 2B, 3A, 3I, 3M.

(2B) Cut one 3" square, then cut ◪.

(3M) Cut one 1½" x 2½" rectangle.

(3I) Cut one 1½" x 4½" rectangle.

(3A) Cut one 3½" x 8½" rectangle.

Caretaker's House

Traditional: Use template patterns 1B, 1F, 4F.

(1B) Cut one 2½" square.

(4F) Cut one 1½" x 4¼" rectangle, then cut off both ends at a 45° ▱

(1F) Cut one 1½" x 3⅞" rectangle, then cut off one end at a 45° ▱

Background

Traditional: Use template patterns 1C, 1D, 2D, 2E, 3B, 3E, 3F, 3J, 3L, 3M, 4B, 4D, 4E.

(2D) Cut one 1⅞" square, then cut ◩ .

(3B) Cut one 3½" x 5½" rectangle.

(2E) Cut one 2⅜" square, then cut ◩ .

(1C) Cut one 2" square.

(3M) Cut one 1½" x 2½" rectangle.

(1D) Cut one 1½" square.

(4E) Cut one 2" x 3½" rectangle.

(3I) Cut one 1½" x 4" rectangle.

(3L) Cut one 1½" x 3" rectangle.

(3F) Cut one 1½" x 14½" rectangle.

(4B) Cut one 2" x 8½" rectangle.

(4D) Cut one 2" x 12" rectangle.

(3E) Cut one 1½" x 9½" rectangle.

Ground

Traditional: Use template pattern 4A.

(4A) Cut one 2" x 9½" rectangle.

PIECING AND PRESSING

The arrows indicate which way to press.

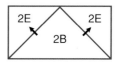

PRESS SEAM OPEN

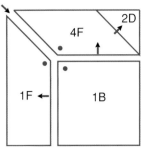

The technique required to piece the caretaker's house is called the Y-seam. Mark your units on the wrong side, ¼" in from the edge, as shown. You must start and stop your stitching <u>only</u> at the dot.

Setting

1. If you are duplicating my quilt, lay the strips out as shown. Cut two blue strips 1½" x 40½" for the two side inner borders.

2. This quilt is constructed of blocks which are multiples of 2". When you put it together, approach it like a jigsaw puzzle. If you have designed your own regatta, lay out your blocks attractively, then sew them together. (Some people are more comfortable if they cut pieces of graph paper to scale and lay them out on paper first.) If your blocks refuse to set in straight units, don't be afraid to use the Y-seam to complete the construction.

3. Sew on the side inner border.

4. Sew on the 4" pinwheels and sawtooth star as your last border.

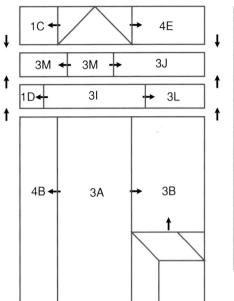

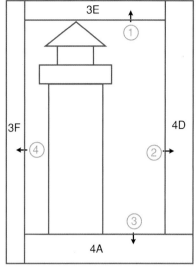

Congratulations, your efforts have paid off! Your sailboat quilt is now ready to layer, baste, and quilt.

CHERRY BASKET

This quilt is 72" x 72" and contains thirty-six 9"
cherry baskets and sixty 4½" postage stamp baskets.
Skill Level: Intermediate to Advanced

*E*very summer when I was a child, we would spend a few weeks with my grandparents in Door County, Wisconsin. We were really lucky if our visit occurred during cherry harvest. When I saw the cherry fabric I knew what quilt I had to make. The challenge came in working with so much pink. My salvation was the little green baskets. I pulled out my color wheel (see page 17) and found that the complement of pink is green. Green made the pink baskets appear richer. *Key*: When a quilt becomes stagnant from an overdose of one color group, try putting in a shot of color from across the color wheel. I have learned there is always a way to get even the most difficult blocks to sing. Just keep looking, and open yourself to new possibilities. By the way, I can still capture the smells and tastes of Grandpa's orchard.

The cherry baskets were pieced from sixteen different pink fabrics, from cotton-candy pink to rich burgundy. In the green outer border are over twenty different greens. This might be a time to look into your personal fabric collection and make a basket quilt, using fabrics in a color you have in over-abundance. Remember to check your local quilt shop for additional pieces: this can make old fabric look updated. *Key*: By using fabrics collected from season to season, your quilt will become more exciting as the different color variations and prints are used together.

Cherry and postage stamp baskets have a strong direction. When you rotate the blocks and join them, interesting positive/negative shapes appear. At the bases of the cherry baskets, a diamond is formed. I repeated diamonds in the inner border; also, by rotating the postage stamp outer border, I formed half-diamonds. *Key*: Look for secondary images when the blocks are set together, and repeat that shape if possible. After making your harvest of baskets, try arranging them differently. You might like your way even better.

Fabric Requirements

White background: 5 yards
Print inner border: ½ yard

The following fabric requirements are the *total* amount of yardage needed to complete your quilt. See General Instructions: Yardage, page 23.

Warning: Unfortunately, there is waste with the basket fabric, as the bias handles take a large diagonal cut. I save these leftover pieces in a box marked "scraps." These scraps become pieces of gold in later projects.

Pink baskets: 2½ yards (The cuts of fabric must be at least ¼ yard in order to be wide enough for the bias handles.)

Green baskets: 1½ yards (The cuts of fabric must be at least ⅛ yard in order to be wide enough for the bias handles.)

Backing: 4½ yards

4½" Postage Stamp Basket

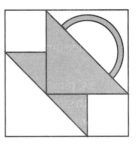

Cherry Basket
Hand quilted by Elke Torgersen

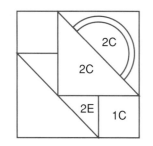

The following cutting numbers are for *one* postage stamp basket. (See General Instructions: Cutting, page 23.)

CUTTING

Traditional: Use template patterns 1C, 2C, 2E.

Postage Stamp Basket

(2C) Cut one 3⅞" square, then cut ◻. (Save the other half-square triangle to cut your bias handle.)

(2E) Cut one 2⅜" square, then cut ◻.

Handle: Cut a 1" strip off the bias edge of the extra triangle. Press in half lengthwise. Note that the ends of the bias handle are not even.

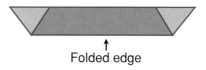

↑
Folded edge

Background

(2C) Cut one 3⅞" square, then cut ◻.

Staystitch one of the triangles ⅛" in on the bias edge. This will keep it from stretching when you sew on the handle.

(1C) Cut two 2" squares.

PIECING AND PRESSING

Use pattern 2C for handle placement. Trace onto your fabric

with a removable marking tool. (Always test your tool on a scrap of the fabric to make sure the mark comes out.)

Hand or machine appliqué the bias handle onto the staystitched background piece 2C. (See drawing of this on page 32.) *Caution:* Match the right side of the background fabric to the longest right side of the bias handle, folded edge to the inside. Flip the handle up over the stitched edge and whipstitch down the outside finished edge.

The arrows indicate which way to press.

The ^ indicates which edge or point to line up.

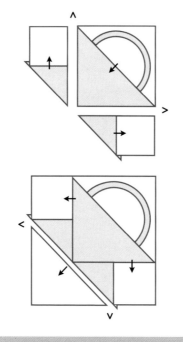

9" Cherry Basket

The following cutting numbers are for *one* cherry basket. *Hint:* Even though triangles 5E and 2E are the same size, they are cut differently to ensure that the straight of grain is kept on the outside edge.

CUTTING

Traditional: Use template patterns 2C, 2E, 2G, 4C, 5E.

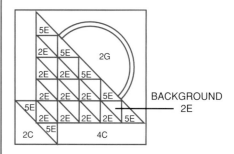

Cherry Basket

(5E) Cut two 3⅜" squares, then cut ⊠. This leaves the outside edge on the straight of grain.

(2E) Cut five 2⅜" squares, then cut ◻.

Handle: Cut a bias strip 1⅛" x 12". Press in half lengthwise. (No template pattern given.)

Background

(2E) Cut five 2⅜" squares, then cut ◻.

(4C) Cut two 6½" x 2" rectangles.

(2C) Cut one 3⅞" square, then cut ◻.

(2G) Cut one 8⅜" square, then cut ◻.

Staystitch the bias edge ⅛" on both the triangles of 2G. This will keep it from stretching when you sew on the handle. Save the extra triangle for your next basket.

PIECING AND PRESSING

The arrows indicate which way to press.

The ^ indicates which edge or point to line up.

1. Hand or machine appliqué the bias handle to the staystitched

2G. Use pattern 2G for handle placement. Trace onto your fabric with a removable marking tool.

2. Sew the ten basket units of 2E to background 2E. Press to basket color 2E.

3. Assemble in rows and units, as shown.

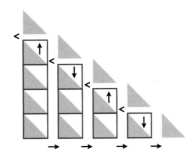

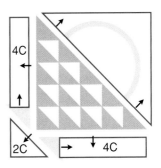

Inner border
(2¼" finished on point
Cherry Square units)

Traditional: Use template patterns 2A, 1E.

(1E) Cut one hundred and eight 2⅛" squares of print fabric.

(2A) Cut two hundred and sixteen 2" squares of background fabric, then cut ◲. Piece and press.

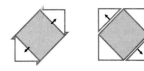

Setting

Cut two inner background strips 2¾" x 54½" each for sides.

Cut two inner background strips 2¾" x 59" each for top and bottom.

1. Lay out your blocks as shown.
2. Join the blocks together in a straight set.
3. Sew on the inner background strips.
4. Sew on the squares of the inner border.
5. Sew on the 4½" postage stamp baskets as your last border.

Congratulations: your efforts have paid off! Your basket quilt is now ready to layer, baste, and quilt.

 *About the Author*

Alex Anderson's love affair with quiltmaking began in 1978, when she completed her Grandmother's Flower Garden quilt as part of her work toward a degree in art at San Francisco State University. Her study of graphic design in fiber inspired in her a deep respect and admiration for Amish quilts, and they became the springboard for Alex's quiltmaking, with their strong visual impact and sensitive intricacy of quilting design. Over the years, her central focus has rested upon star quilts and an intense appreciation of traditional surface design.

For more than a decade, Alex's quilts have been displayed in one-woman shows and have won prizes in group shows. She has lectured to numerous guilds, taught frequently at leading conferences, and offered classes at several different quilt shops. Her quilts have also been shown in magazines, including an article specifically about her works, and her quilts have been seen widely in a number of books by Diana McClun, Laura Nownes, Margaret Peters, and Mary Coyne Penders. She also worked with her father to develop his company, Sladky Quilt Frames.

Alex lives in Livermore, California, with her husband, two children, three cats, one dog, two fish, and the challenges of suburban life.

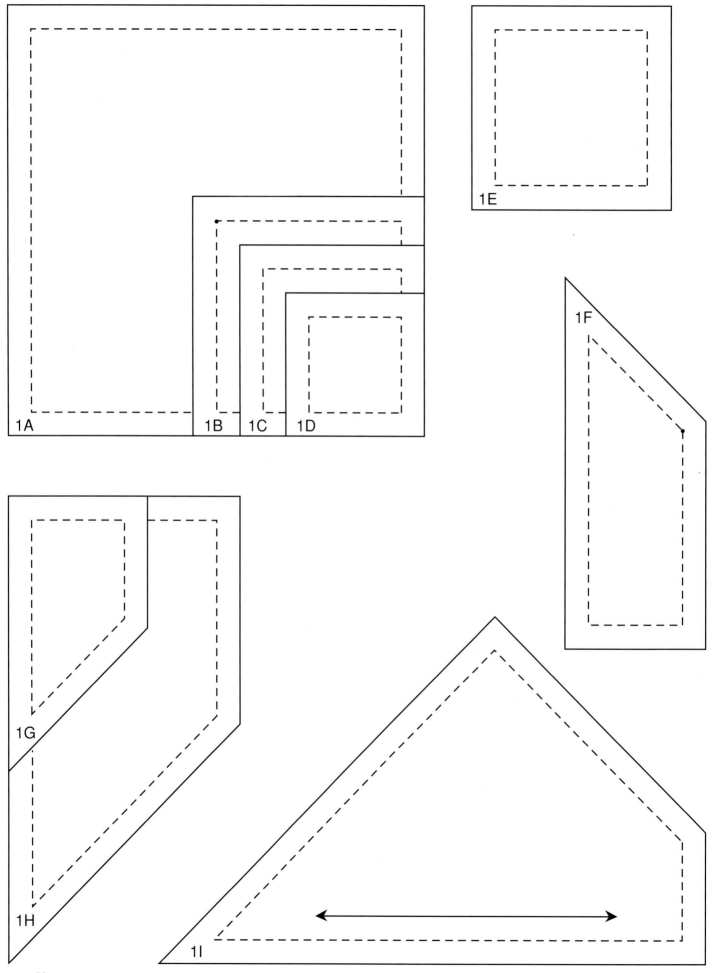

1A

1B 1C 1D

1E

1F

1G

1H

1I

58

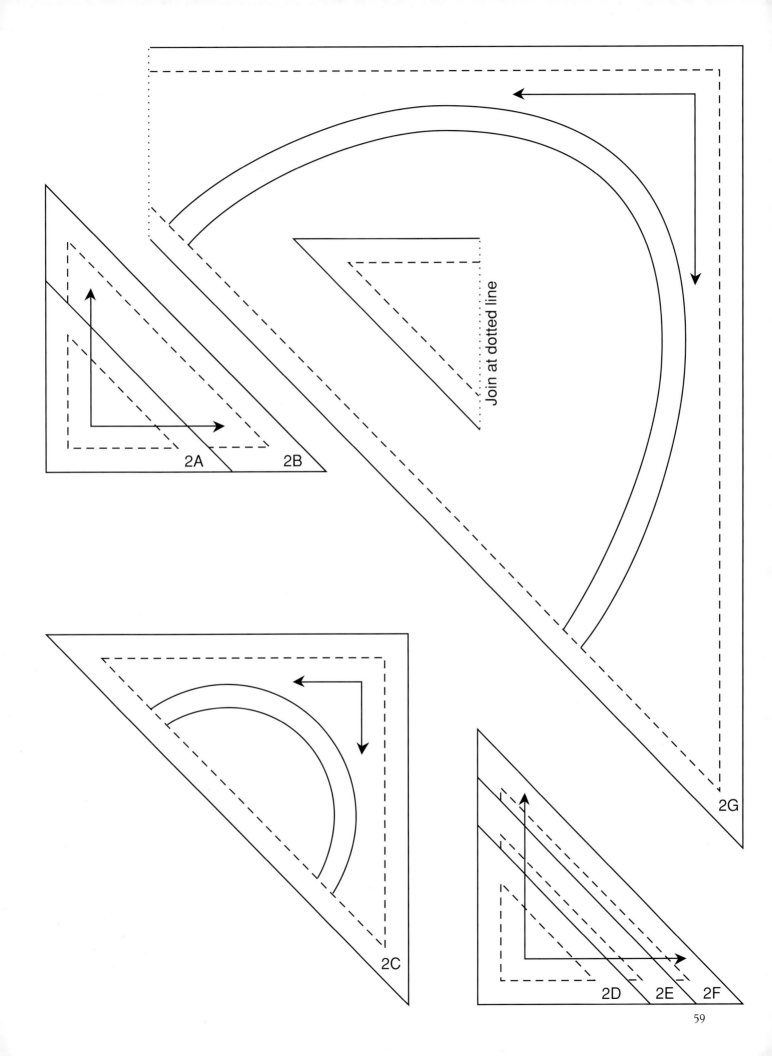

Join at dotted line

2A 2B

2C

2D 2E 2F

2G

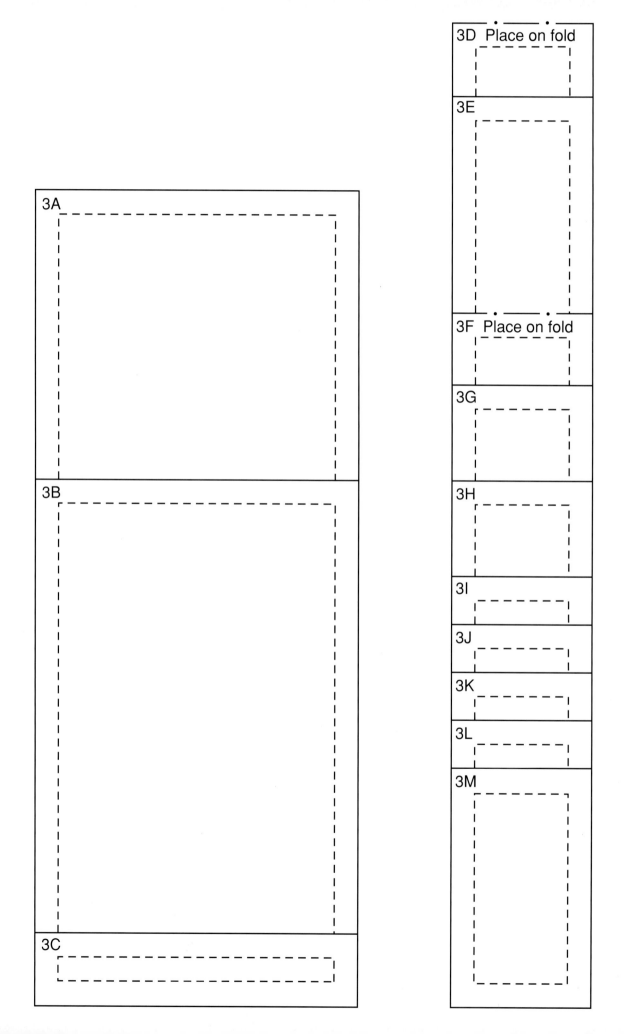

3A

3B

3C

3D Place on fold

3E

3F Place on fold

3G

3H

3I

3J

3K

3L

3M

60

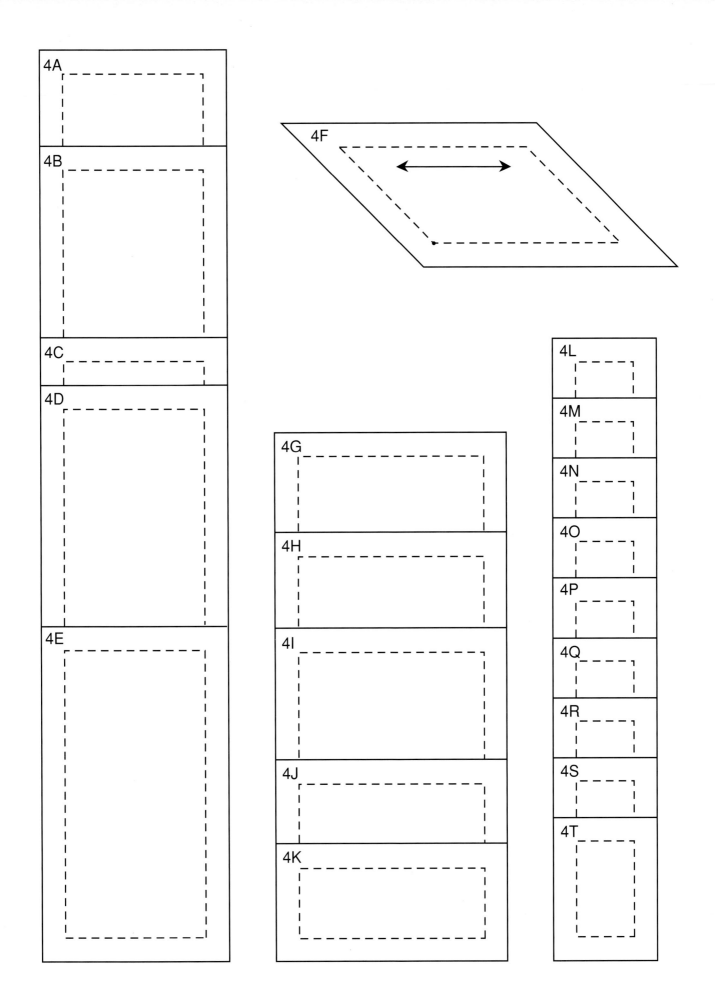

4A

4B

4C

4D

4E

4F

4G

4H

4I

4J

4K

4L

4M

4N

4O

4P

4Q

4R

4S

4T

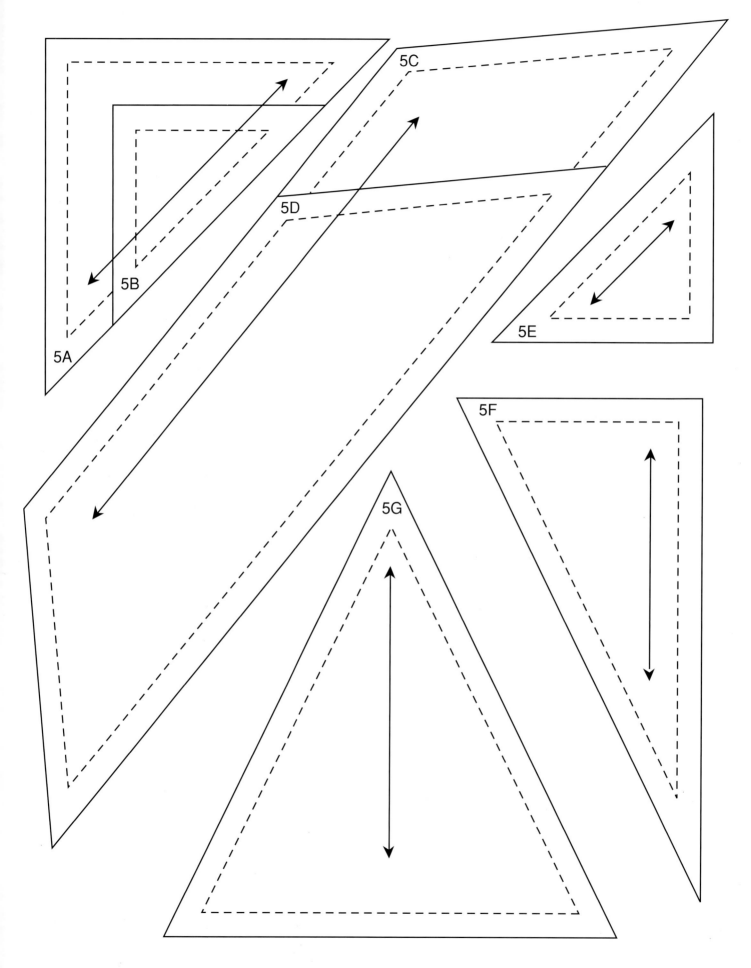

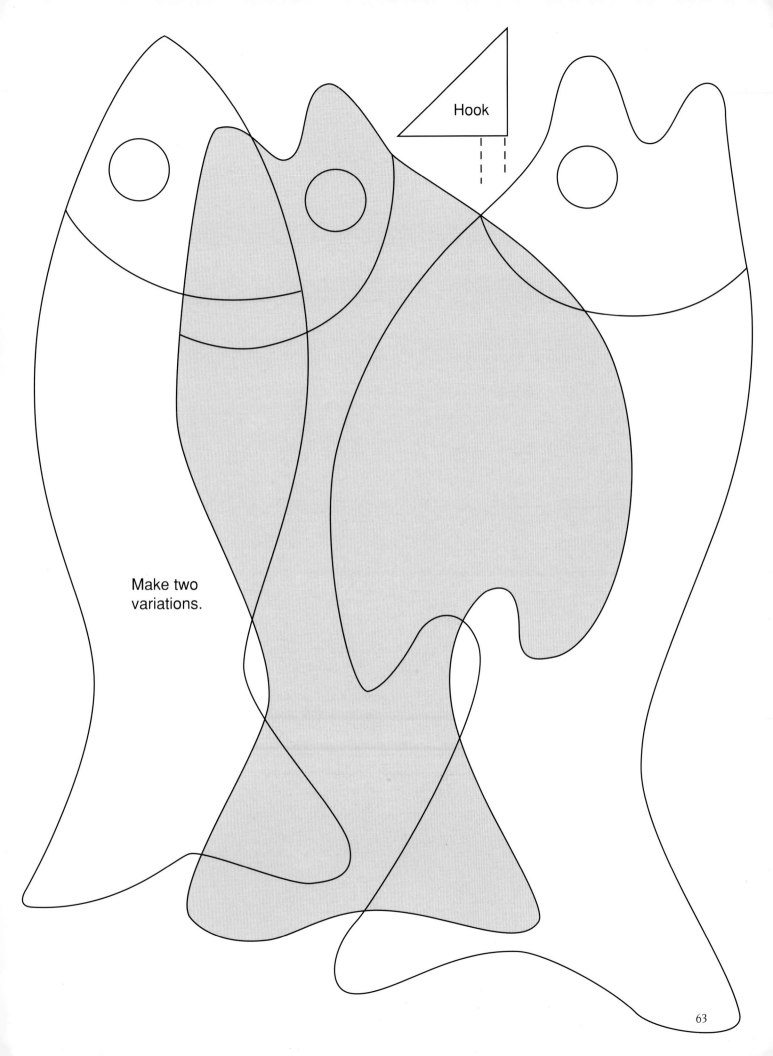

Hook

Make two
variations.

63

Other Fine Quilting Books
from C&T Publishing

An Amish Adventure, Roberta Horton

Appliqué 12 Easy Ways! Elly Sienkiewicz

Appliqué 12 Borders and Medallions! Elly Sienkiewicz

The Art of Silk Ribbon Embroidery, Judith Montano

Baltimore Album Quilts, Historic Notes and Antique Patterns, Elly Sienkiewicz

Baltimore Album Revival! Historic Quilts in the Making. The Catalog of C&T Publishing's Quilt Show and Contest, Elly Sienkiewicz

Baltimore Beauties and Beyond (2 Volumes), Elly Sienkiewicz

The Best From Gooseberry Hill: Patterns For Stuffed Animals & Dolls, Kathy Pace

Boston Commons Quilt, Blanche Young and Helen Young Frost

Calico and Beyond, Roberta Horton

A Celebration of Hearts, Jean Wells and Marina Anderson

Christmas Traditions From the Heart, Margaret Peters

Christmas Traditions From the Heart, Volume Two, Margaret Peters

A Colorful Book, Yvonne Porcella

Colors Changing Hue, Yvonne Porcella

Crazy Quilt Handbook, Judith Montano

Crazy Quilt Odyssey, Judith Montano

Design a Baltimore Album Quilt! Elly Sienkiewicz

Dimensional Appliqué—Baskets, Blooms & Borders, Elly Sienkiewicz

Elegant Stitches, Judith Baker Montano

Fantastic Figures: Ideas & Techniques Using the New Clays, Susanna Oroyan

Flying Geese Quilt, Blanche Young and Helen Young Frost

14,287 Pieces of Fabrics and Other Poems, Jean Ray Laury

Friendship's Offering, Susan McKelvey

Happy Trails, Pepper Cory

Heirloom Machine Quilting, Harriet Hargrave

Imagery on Fabric, Jean Ray Laury

Irish Chain Quilt, Blanche Young and Helen Young Frost

Isometric Perspective, Katie Pasquini-Masopust

Landscapes & Illusions, Joen Wolfrom

Let's Make Waves, Marianne Fons and Liz Porter

The Magical Effects of Color, Joen Wolfrom

Mariner's Compass, Judy Mathieson

Mastering Machine Appliqué, Harriet Hargrave

Memorabilia Quilting, Jean Wells

The New Lone Star Handbook, Blanche Young and Helen Young Frost

NSA Series: Bloomin' Creations, Jean Wells

NSA Series: Holiday Magic, Jean Wells

NSA Series: Hometown, Jean Wells

NSA Series: Fans, Hearts, & Folk Art, Jean Wells

Pattern Play, Doreen Speckmann

Perfect Pineapples, Jane Hall and Dixie Haywood

Picture This, Jean Wells and Marina Anderson

Pieced Clothing, Yvonne Porcella

Pieced Clothing Variations, Yvonne Porcella

Plaids and Stripes, Roberta Horton

PQME Series: Basket Quilt, Jean Wells

PQME Series: Bear's Paw Quilt, Jean Wells

PQME Series: Country Bunny Quilt, Jean Wells

PQME Series: Milky Way Quilt, Jean Wells

PQME Series: Nine-Patch Quilt, Jean Wells

PQME Series: Pinwheel Quilt, Jean Wells

PQME Series: Sawtooth Star Quilt, Jean Wells

PQME Series: Stars & Hearts Quilt, Jean Wells

Patchwork Quilts Made Easy, Jean Wells (co-published with Rodale)

Quilts, Quilts, and More Quilts! Diana McClun and Laura Nownes

Recollections, Judith Montano

Stitching Free: Easy Machine Pictures, Shirley Nilsson

Story Quilts, Mary Mashuta

Symmetry: A Design System for Quiltmakers, Ruth B. McDowell

3 Dimensional Design, Katie Pasquini

A Treasury of Quilt Labels, Susan McKelvey

Trip Around the World Quilts, Blanche Young and Helen Young Frost

Virginia Avery's Hats, A Heady Affair

Virginia Avery's Nifty Neckwear

Visions: The Art of the Quilt, Quilt San Diego

Visions: Quilts, Layers of Excellence, Quilt San Diego

Whimsical Animals, Miriam Gourley

Wearable Art for Real People, Mary Mashuta

For more information write for a free catalog from
C&T Publishing
P.O. Box 1456
Lafayette, CA 94549
(1-800-284-1114)